The Bazaar Handbook

The Bazaar Handbook

Jackie Vermeer and Marian Lariviere Frew

PHOTOGRAPHY BY DUANE DAVIS

VAN NOSTRAND REINHOLD COMPANY
New York   Cincinnati   Toronto   London   Melbourne

All color and black and white photographs were taken by Duane Davis with the exception of Figure 2-8, 2-10, and 2-36, which were taken by Paul McMaster.

All drawings and illustrations were done by the authors.

Copyright © 1980 by Litton Educational Publishing, Inc.
Library of Congress Catalog Card Number 80—14466
ISBN 0-442-22652-7

Printed in the United States of America
Designed by Loudan Enterprises

Published in 1980 by Van Nostrand Reinhold Company
A division of Litton Educational Publishing, Inc.
135 West 50th Street, New York, NY 10020, U.S.A.

Van Nostrand Reinhold Limited
1410 Birchmount Road
Scarborough, Ontario M1P 2E7, Canada

Van Nostrand Reinhold Australia Pty. Ltd.
17 Queen Street
Mitcham, Victoria 3132, Australia

Van Nostrand Reinhold Company Limited
Molly Millars Lare
Wokingham, Berkshire, England

16 15 14 13 12 11 10 9 8 7 6 5 4 3 2 1

Library of Congress Cataloging in Publication Data
Vermeer, Jackie.
    The bazaar handbook.

    Includes index.
    1. Handicraft.   2. Bazaars, Charitable.
I. Frew, Marian Lariviere, joint author.   II. Title.
TT157.V47   745.5   80-14466
ISBN 0-442-22652-7

Dedication

TO LOU AND DICK ·

Contents

Acknowledgments

To Alice Ray, Ann Lubbers, Carolin Vermeer, Janet Vermeer, Joy Reeb, Joyce Lawrence, Leigh Lubbers, Lena Harting, and Peggy Mahler we wish to express our sincere appreciation for the ideas and good wishes that they shared with us. We are grateful to "Cap" Davis for his outstanding photography, as well as for his patience and sense of humor.

We thank our children, David, Kristin, Todd, and Neal, for their enthusiasm and interest in this book. A special thank you to our husbands, Lou and Dick, who have helped in so many ways to make this all possible. Most of all, we thank each other for the hard work, the understanding, the laughter, and the good times we have always shared.

# Introduction

Bazaars are thought of primarily as fund-raising activities, yet the personal satisfaction gained by those involved with bazaars is an equally rewarding pastime. Working in a group provides the opportunity to renew old friendships and to develop new ones. Like the quilting bee, these work sessions are a time of sharing work, ideas, traditions, and good cheer.

The ideas presented in this book are easily made with common materials. We have tried to present a broad selection of items to appeal to a variety of individual interests and age groups. We believe there is something here for everyone. These projects may be used as they are, or may serve as inspirations for new creations. Don't be afraid to experiment; you might end up creating something altogether new and exciting. Whether you use the ideas as presented or experiment with some original ones, we hope you will enjoy using the projects and suggestions presented here.

Bazaars provide a social aspect to community life that is both fun and rewarding. Hopefully, the ideas presented here will aid the newcomer in getting started, and will provide the more experienced with new ideas. See you at the bazaar!

 **Tips for Your Bazaar**

A successful bazaar requires advance planning, organization, and the cooperation of all members of the group. The following tips and suggestions will aid you in preparing for your bazaar.

Start planning early so that all members have ample time to complete their assignments, thereby avoiding a last minute rush to finish things. Good organization will result in an efficient and pleasant work procedure. If you are well prepared and have taken care of all the details ahead of time, you will avoid frustrations. The venture should be enjoyable, successful, and rewarding for everyone.

Early Planning

Whether you are planning a large bazaar or a moderately sized one, careful planning will greatly affect its success, and whether this is a group or an individual effort, early planning is essential. A bazaar chairperson should be selected, and this person should choose a chairperson for each group of workers. Each group chairperson should then post a sign-up sheet, so that each member of the organization can choose the group in which he or she wishes to participate.

Each group should submit to the bazaar chairperson a list of materials and the quantities needed for the projects. By combining these lists, it may be possible to purchase some of the materials in larger quantities at lower prices. It might be best to have one person purchase all the materials. This should be someone who enjoys shopping around to find the best price.

Preplanning allows ample time to choose and construct the projects and also provides the opportunity for you to take advantage of any needed materials that may be on sale during the year or that will have to be collected. Throughout the year, all members should save usable throwaways, such as meat trays, small paper bags, gift boxes, fabric remnants, and trim. Buying the necessary materials on sale will greatly reduce the expense of the items to be sold, and, needless to say, that is an important consideration.

Many kinds of natural materials are only collectable at certain times of the year, so you would do well to keep the bazaar in mind when these materials are available. When gathering natural materials, you might even collect "extras," which you could then trade with a friend in a different geographical area, thereby increasing your varieties of dried materials. Also, don't overlook the possibility of selling interesting or unusual seed pods as items in and of themselves.

Organizing the Work

The making of the projects should be divided among several groups. This is the most efficient method of producing a quantity of bazaar items and it also allows for the individual to choose the group according to his or her interests. Each group assumes the responsibility for collecting the materials necessary for its projects and for getting those projects finished on time. The group chairperson and his or her members will need to plan work schedules convenient to the other members of the group. For example, if one member is only able to work a few evenings, that person might be assigned the task of cutting out certain project pieces. These pieces could then be turned over to other members who can work together constructing the project in an assembly-line fashion.

As you will discover, there are ways to save time and materials when making large quantities of any project. For example, when cutting a large number of similar pieces, it is a good idea to have several patterns of the same piece to use in the cutting process. Take for example, the tree project on page 19. By using several tree patterns you will con-serve both materials and energy. Lay the first tree pattern right side up, the next pattern upside down, and so on. By doing this you will get fifteen tree backgrounds, each 18 inches wide, from an 8-foot length of Masonite. Always place patterns as close together as possible so as to avoid unnecessary waste. When all of the pieces for a project are ready, the construction should be set up as an assembly line—each person being responsible for one step in the production.

Obviously, you should try to assign jobs according to the individual talents and interests of the group members. Furthermore, if a member has a special talent in an unusual craft, such as quilling, wood carving, or tole painting, they might be willing to practice their art for short periods of time during the bazaar. This would attract shoppers and might help increase sales.

As it approaches the date of the bazaar, a schedule should be worked out so that members of the group can take turns working at the booth. When people are assigned to a booth for which they made projects, they often end up being effective salespersons, having had involvement with the items being sold. The member should be told to keep records of sales transactions. The records are necessary for the group's cost analysis, and may be important, depending on sales tax regulations in your area.

What to Offer

The ideal bazaar should offer something for everyone, but special consideration should be given to young shoppers, both for their own enjoyment and to entertain them so that their parents' shopping trip will be more pleasant. If at all possible, one booth should be set aside especially for children. This booth could include inexpensive items that children could buy for themselves, gifts for children, and entertaining games children can play while parents are shopping. In the event that a special booth cannot be set aside for this purpose, a number of small, inexpensive items should be available somewhere for them to purchase.

At every bazaar there should be a selection of gifts for holidays and other special occasions. A Christmas gift could be a wall hanging or a pine cone wreath. A variety of Christmas decorations for the tree or to be used as package ties, such as hazelnut elves, felt boots with a candy cane tucked in each, or knitted bells, should be offered. A group of stocking stuffers might include such items as a special tree ornament, a bookmarker, a small doll, or a puppet.

Shoppers are on the lookout for gift items for all occasions and it is a good idea to keep some suggestions in mind, to help them. Dried flower wall hangings or pot holders make excellent hostess or thank you gifts. A bib or a small

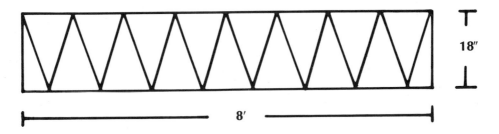

quilt is perfect for a baby shower gift. A candleholder or a basket of dried flowers would make a nice Mother's Day present and fathers enjoy key tags or special covered matchboxes. Suitably decorated napkins and napkin rings would make a nice gift on Valentine's Day. Home-baked goodies are always a thoughtful present for someone who doesn't have time to bake, and plants make nice remembrances for shut-ins or simply for plant lovers. Children always like to receive toys, and newlyweds might welcome a cookbook.

Plants are always popular selling items. Seeds and cuttings should be started well in advance to ensure healthy, attractive plants. Small plants could be sold in Styrofoam cups (gaily decorated), plastic glasses, cut bottles, or unused cups or bowls. Larger plants could be sold in coffee cans, canisters, or flower pots, any of which can be dressed up using adhesive-backed paper, florist's foil, or even a square of brightly colored fabric tied with a perky bow.

Baked goods are a standard fare at bazaars. To allow for more variety and ease of handling, small portions should be offered. Try baking yeast or nut breads in small individual loaf pans. Small pies can be baked in 4-inch disposable pie tins. A dozen cookies, six cupcakes, or one-half pound of candy can be packaged in Styrofoam meat trays and covered with plastic wrap. These small portions are particularly appealing to those people who live alone or to those who would like to purchase a variety of baked goods. Single portions should also be available for those who like to snack while shopping. Things that are particularly adaptable to selling singly are caramel apples, popcorn balls, lollipops, doughnuts, bags of popcorn, cupcakes, and large cookies.

Keeping Costs Down

The cost of materials can be kept to a minimum by shopping carefully. Particularly watch for sales on such items as Dacron batting, remnants, yarn, felt, and beads. Ask friends and neighbors to save fabric scraps and lumber scraps. Check garage sales, rummage sales, and thrift shops for fabric, edgings, craft supplies, unusual plant containers, and baskets. By consolidating the materials lists of all the groups, you can purchase enough of each material to take advantage of lower prices. Also, when you know in advance what materials will be needed, you can take advantage of off-season sales on particular items. This is particularly true after Christmas when many holiday supplies are on sale.

Setting the Prices

The price to be charged for the items will have to be decided by the group making the item. While there is no "rule of thumb" for this, there are a number of points to be taken into consideration when setting your prices. The first thing to consider is *the cost of the materials needed to make the item.* You should use the regular retail cost even if some or all of the materials were donated. The next consideration is *how much time was required to make the item.* This is important even though you may not be able to charge an adequate price for the time involved. Also, *find out what items of similar quality sell for in retail stores* and try to make your prices competitive. Finally, stop and ask yourself *what would you be willing to pay for this item.*

Don't overlook the value of good salesmanship at your bazaar. A friendly, helpful person will outsell the high-pressure salesperson or the one who doesn't say anything at all. All the items should be individually priced, but it is also a good idea to have a special quantity price. An example of this: one dollar and fifty cents each or three for four dollars. This kind of pricing is often enough to encourage shoppers to buy several items rather than just one.

The Importance of Color

When making items for a bazaar, color is an important factor to keep in mind. Remember that you are trying to appeal to a wide variety of individual tastes and, therefore, very specialized color schemes will have limited appeal. When selecting compatible colors, use the following color scheme suggestions as a guide:

Monochromatic scheme: Tints and shades of a single color.

Earth tones: Rusts, browns, burnt orange, beige, and moss green.

Cool colors: Blues and greens.

Warm colors: Red, oranges, and yellows.

Touches of white or black may be added to any of the above schemes as accent colors.

You will have greater success selling seasonal items if you use the colors that are primarily associated with that particular season or holiday. For example, Halloween decorations are traditionally orange, yellow, and black; red, green, and white are the colors associated with Christmas. This does not mean that other colors should not be used, but simply that the traditional colors associated with special occasions will appeal to a greater number of people.

Setting Up the Booths

The display arrangement at each booth is an important part of selling. Before you can plan your display, you need to know the amount of available space, the position of your booth, and whether or not tables are provided. The table should be covered with a cloth; a simple white sheet works well. Group similar items together—all the Christmas ornaments together, all the baked goods together, and so on. Only display five or six samples of an item. Then, as these are sold, replenish them from your supply. Keep things neatly arranged on the table and avoid any kind of a cluttered look. For some items you may wish to have additional display space—a background board on which to hang pictures or a rack on which to display a coverlet.

If items are not to be individually price-tagged, then price lists should be posted in places convenient for both the buyer and the seller.

The workers in the booth should be supplied with some type of cash box containing ample change. Adequately sized paper bags should be available as a convenience for the customer.

After the Bazaar

After the close of the bazaar, it's helpful for the group to get together for an evaluation. Things to be discussed should include best-selling items, most profitable items, net profit, problem areas, suggestions for improvement, and committee assignments for the next bazaar.

How to Use the Patterns

Patterns are provided for many of the projects given here so that they may be easily reproduced. The patterns are presented in two ways—either actual size or reduced. The patterns that have been reduced are shown on a grid, or squared background. On all of the grids, 1 square equals 1 inch. To make the proper size pattern draw straight lines 1 inch apart in both horizontal and vertical directions on a large piece of butcher or kraft paper. This will create a grid on which to draw the pattern in its proper size. Following the pattern in the book, draw the pattern, square by square on your grid. Two pages of 1-inch grids have been provided for you in the back of the book.

If you want to increase the size of the pattern, simply increase the size of your squares. For example, if you want to double the size, draw 2-inch squares, instead of 1-inch squares. To decrease, you would make smaller squares.

To reproduce the patterns that are actual size, you simply trace from the book, using tracing paper. Then transfer the design to a heavy paper or posterboard, using carbon paper. You will want to use heavy paper or posterboard in order to make a sturdy pattern that can be used many times. This method can also be used to transfer to wood, as the carbon paper will provide a good guide for cutting. After cutting, any blue line that remains can be easily sanded off. When transferring the patterns onto fabric, do so on the back side of the fabric so that any line that remains after cutting will not show on the finished product. Be sure to turn the pattern over for use on the back side. In some cases this is not important, but, if you are doing a project with lettering, it is very important. If you don't turn the patterns over, the letters will be backward. Always check this after cutting the first time to make sure of the results.

2 Christmas Creations

Traditionally, bazaars are held in the fall for a simple reason—they provide the opportunity for early Christmas shopping. These local fairs are often the best source for shoppers who are looking for new and different kinds of Christmas decorations and ornaments, as well as handmade gifts and toys for the special people on their Christmas list.

Bazaars afford an excellent opportunity for individuals and groups to market their creations. This seasonal event is a good fund-raising activity for organizations, as well as for part-time craftsmen.

Natural materials are in keeping with the Christmas spirit and lend themselves to traditional types of decorations. For these kinds of decorations there are a great variety of usable materials available. The first thing that comes to mind is pine cones. However, don't limit yourself to these. Consider also whole nuts, dried fruit pits, and seed pods. These additional materials add interest because of their varying textures and colors. Keep in mind that it is important to allow all these materials to dry thoroughly before beginning a project.

Pine Cone Wreaths

If you'd like to work with natural materials, a fairly simple beginning project is a wreath, and pine cones are particularly well suited to this use. The materials listed here will enable you to make one wreath.

MATERIALS

1 sheet of heavy cardboard, 7 by 7 inches
scissors or utility knife
red ribbon, ½-inch wide, 16 inches
staple gun and staples
adhesive-backed picture hanger
brown linoleum paste (or other dark color)
putty knife
9 pine cones, about 3 inches in length
18 tiny pine cones or sections of pine cones
spray lacquer

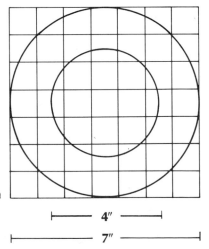

DIRECTIONS

1. With scissors or a utility knife, cut a cardboard ring, using the pattern given here.
2. Cut the ribbon into four 4-inch lengths. Staple three of the ribbon sections to the back side of the cardboard ring, near the bottom.
3. Staple a folded 4-inch ribbon near the top.
4. Attach the picture hanger.
5. Liberally apply linoleum paste, using a putty knife, to the front side of the ring.
6. Arrange the larger cones evenly spaced around the ring, then fill in all spaces with the tiny cones or sections.
7. Press all cones down firmly to be sure they are well anchored in the paste.
8. Spray with lacquer for a glossy finish, and let dry for at least 24 hours.

Scale: 1 square = 1 inch

7"

4"

7"

16

A larger wreath can be made in the same manner, using a 12-inch circle and removing a 6-inch circle from the center. For this size wreath you will require large pine cones plus a variety of smaller ones to fill in the spaces. Use 2-inch-wide red ribbon for this wreath.

Pine Cone Wall Decoration

This lovely wall decoration is made with an assortment of natural materials. For this you will want to include small pine cones and sections of large cones, liquidambar (sweetgum), seed pods, acorns, horse chestnuts, whole peach or apricot pits, and any other suitable dried seed pods. The materials here are for one project.

MATERIALS

1 sheet of Masonite, 12 by 18 inches
   (30 by 45 cm.)
hand or power saw
adhesive-backed picture hanger
brown linoleum paste (or other dark
   color)
putty knife
liquid plastic or lacquer
assorted natural materials
red ribbon, ½-inch wide, 18 inches
red ribbon, 1-inch wide, 36 inches
fine wire

DIRECTIONS

1. With either a hand or power saw, cut the Masonite, using the pattern given here.
2. Attach the picture hanger to the smooth side of the Masonite, leaving the textured side for the front.
3. Liberally apply linoleum paste to the Masonite, using a putty knife.
4. Begin placing all the natural materials on the Masonite, arrange the larger ones first and fill in with the smaller ones. It is important that the background be covered as completely as possible.
5. Press the natural materials into place so they are well anchored in the paste.
6. Spray or brush on liquid plastic or lacquer to bring out the natural colors.
7. Cut and tie the ½-inch-wide ribbon into bows. Intersperse them among the natural materials. Tie the 1-inch-wide ribbon into a large bow and add it to the base of the tree. Attach the bows with fine wire, the ends of which are inserted into the linoleum paste.
8. Allow the finished tree to dry for at least 24 hours.

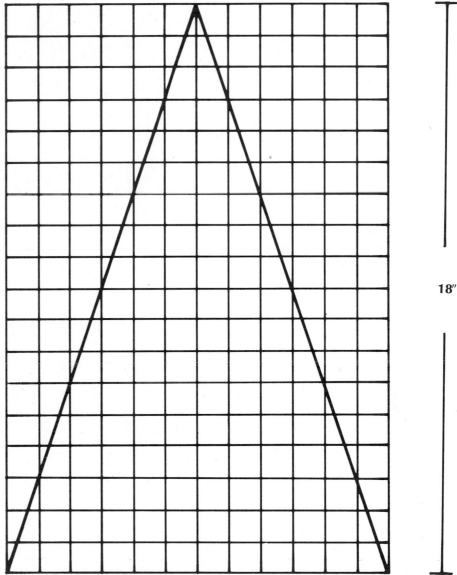

18"

12"

<u>Scale:</u>   **1 square = 1 inch**

19

Simple Nativity Scene

An unusual nativity scene can be constructed from wood scraps and straight clothespins. Here the felt clothing on the figures add a touch of color to the scene. Materials given here are for one scene.

MATERIALS

small pieces of wood paneling
saw
white glue
wood strips, ¾-inch wide
2 straight clothespins
acrylic paint or model airplane enamel
fine brush, #0 or 00
2 small pieces of felt
short lengths of trim or metallic thread
1 slice from a ¾-inch dowel, ⅛-inch thick
bead for manager, ¾-inch long
tiny bead
small fold of cloth
saw dust
toothpick

DIRECTIONS

1. Cut the two pieces of paneling to form background and base of crèche, using hand or power saw. Glue together.
2. Add sections of wood strips for the roof lines, as desired.
3. Cut off both clothespins at an appropriate length to make the figures.
4. Paint faces, using the fine brush.
5. Dress figures in felt and add any desired decorations with trim or metallic thread.
6. Glue the dowel slice on for Mary's halo.
7. Remove a wedge-shaped piece from the large bead to form the manger.
8. Add saw dust, bead head, and cloth blanket to complete the manger.
9. Position figures and manger on the base and glue in place.
10. Add a toothpick for Joseph's staff.

Empty Yarn Cone Decorations

Empty yarn cones provide the base for a variety of colorful Christmas decorations. These cones, which are actually spools for threads and macrame cords, can probably be obtained by asking for them at needlework shops.

The first step in decorating these cones is to cover the surface of the cone. The small cones shown here have been covered with fabric. The tree on the right was covered with red felt, glued in place, and then decorated with white lace, rickrack, and a yarn pom-pom for the top. The other tree was covered with strips of gathered gingham and calico. The strips of material must be 1½ times the circumference of the cone before gathering. After gathering, the strips are

glued in tiers on the cone surface. A circle of rickrack and a glass ball complete the tree.

If you are planning to make a number of these gingham and calico trees, machine gather long strips of fabric using the shirring attachment on your sewing machine. Because it is machine stitched, the desired lengths can be cut without disturbing the gathers.

Another method of covering the cones is to wrap them with brightly colored yarn. To do this paint the lower 2-inch portion of the cone with white glue. The glue will have to be thinned with a little water to achieve a painting consistency. Tuck one end of the yarn under the bottom of the cone and begin

wrapping the yarn around the cone, covering the entire surface from bottom to top. Tuck the yarn end into the opening at the top of the cone. These yarn wrapped cones are now ready to be decorated. Yarn, macaroni, or felt were used to decorate the cones in the photograph here, but you need not be limited by these suggestions—experiment with other possible decorating materials.

The trio of Wise Men make a simple, yet elegant, addition to any Christmas decor. Use the following patterns here to cut the beards, crowns, and jewels for these 9-inch cones. Other sizes will require the patterns to be adjusted accordingly.

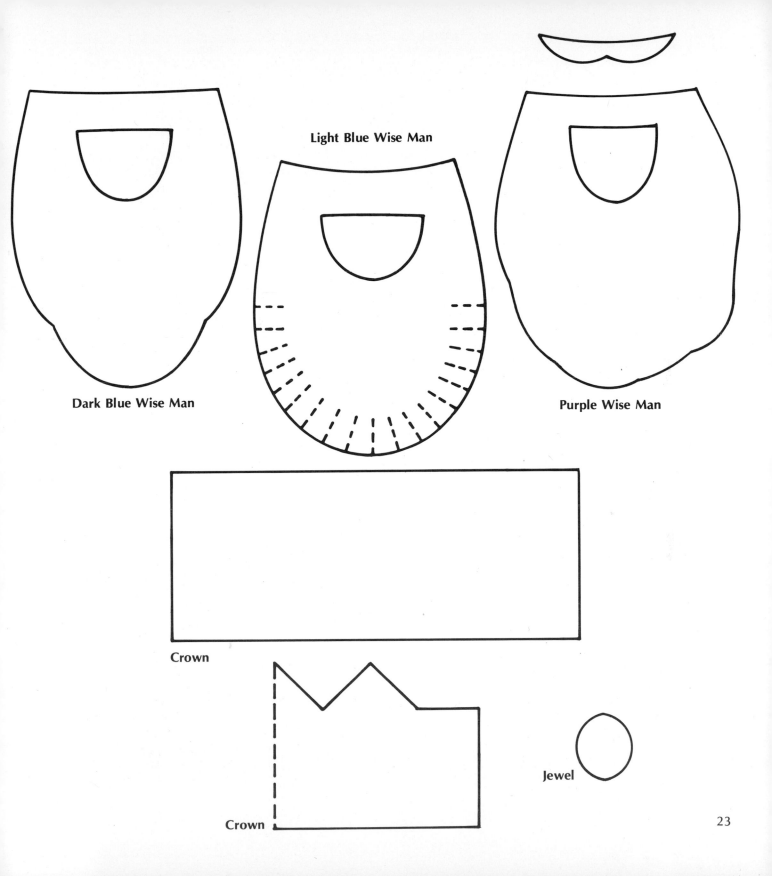

Light Blue Wise Man

Dark Blue Wise Man

Purple Wise Man

Crown

Crown

Jewel

23

Nontraditional Christmas Stockings

Christmas stockings have generally followed a traditional pattern. However, there is no reason why other shapes could not be used. A bazaar shopper might be attracted to a cowboy boot, a sneaker, or a roller skate.

MATERIALS
upholstery or other heavy fabric
naugahyde, vinyl, or oil cloth
scissors
sewing machine
iron-on tape
iron

DIRECTIONS
1. Place the patterns on the fold of your material, as shown by the dotted lines, and cut. Use the upholstery fabric for the upper portion of the boot and the naugahyde for the lower portion.
2. Machine-stitch upper and lower sections together, using a ½-inch seam allowance.
3. With right sides of fabric together, stitch bottom and side seams of the boot closed.
4. Turn boot right side out.
5. Cut the design from iron-on tape and press in place using a pressing cloth.
6. Cut a strip from the heavy material and add a loop at the top of the boot for hanging.

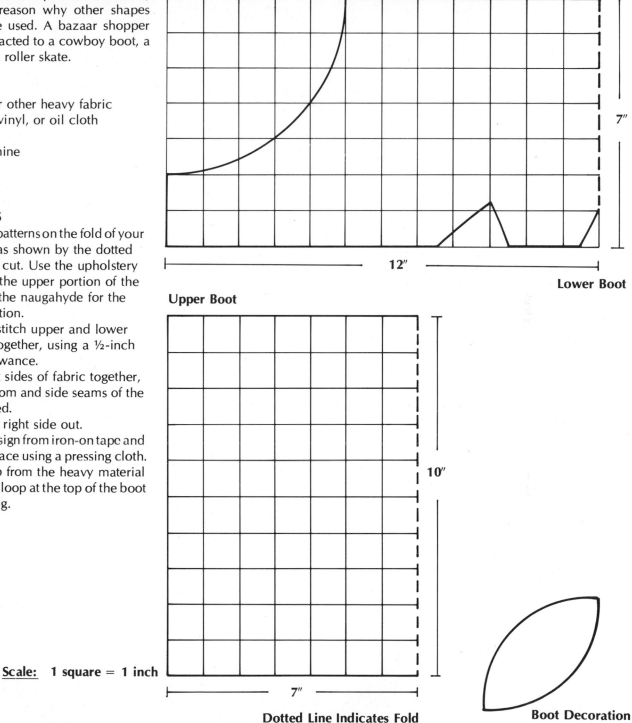

Upper Boot

12"

7"

Lower Boot

10"

7"

Scale: 1 square = 1 inch

Dotted Line Indicates Fold

Boot Decoration

Canvas and bias tape were combined to form the tennis shoe shown, and felt was used to make the roller skate shown on page 28. The eyelets of the tennis shoe, made with an eyelet maker, provide a more authentic appearance and allow for lacing. The roller skate is made entirely of felt, with yarn for the laces. Enlarge the patterns given here or create your own patterns. The ideas presented here are only a few of the possibilities that could be used to make stockings that would appeal to individual interests at a bazaar. Hiking shoes, saddle shoes, penny loafers —the possibilities are endless.

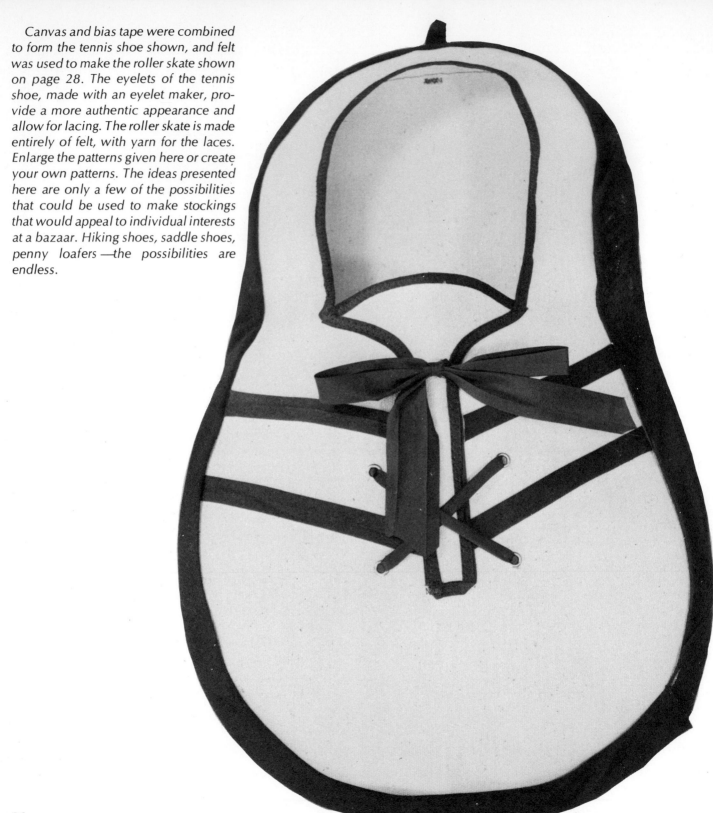

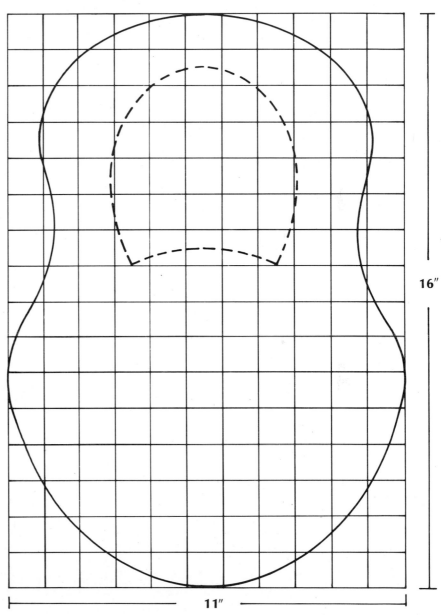

Scale: 1 square = 1 inch

16"

11"

27

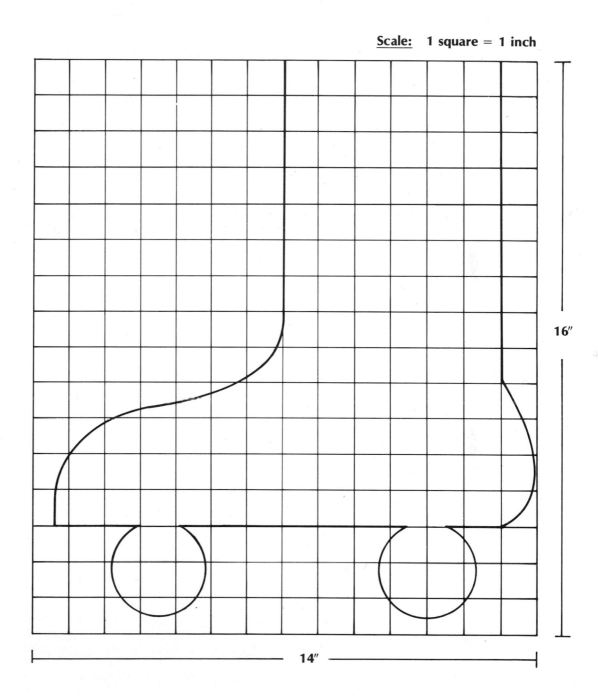

Scale: 1 square = 1 inch

16"

14"

Fabric Wall Hangings

Unique wall hangings are an interesting part of holiday decorating. The following example is a very simple idea for a wall decoration. Materials given are for one hanging.

MATERIALS

green felt, 5¼ by 21 inches
red polka dot fabric, 5 by 20 inches
white felt, 8½ by 39 inches
straight pins
scissors
sewing machine
thread
green yarn pom-pom, 2 inches in diameter
dowel, ⅜ inch in diameter, 12 inches
Optional: permanent green felt-tipped marker or wood stain

DIRECTIONS

1. Cut background letters of green felt using the 5¼-inch letter patterns (the outer letter outline).
2. Cut fabric letters from red polka dot fabric, using 5-inch letter patterns (the inner letter outline).
3. Place fabric letters on top of felt letters and position on white felt background. Place the N 6½ inches from the top of the background piece. Allow 2 inches between each of the other letters. Pin letters in place.
4. Machine-applique the letters to the background by stitching along the edge of the fabric letters using a zigzag stitch.
5. Fold over 1 inch at the top and stitch to form a casing for the dowel.
6. Turn lower corners under to form a V and stitch.
7. Attach a yarn pom-pom at the bottom of the V.
8. If desired, color the dowel with the permanent felt-tipped marker or stain it with wood stain.
9. Insert the dowel for hanging.

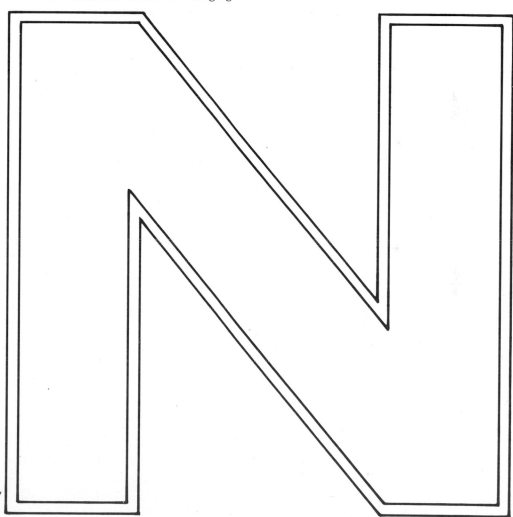

Inner Letter = 5"
Outer Letter = 5¼"

C-1

An appliquéd afghan such as this one can be made easily, especially when the work is organized in an assembly-line fashion. See instructions on page 81.

C-2.

Instructions for this and other cut-paper designs can be found on page 64.

C-3.

Copper blanks make interesting key chains and there's one here to suit almost anyone's taste. See page 97 for details.

C-4.

This brightly colored tote bag will attract shoppers and is very easy to make. Instructions are on page 85.

C-5.

Decorative, easy-to-make paper stars are wonderful, inexpensive Christmas ornaments. Instructions are on page 38.

C-6.

Gay holiday banners such as this one not only sell well, but help to dress up the bazaar. See instructions on page 30.

C-7.

Natural materials such as pine cones lend themselves perfectly for use in holiday decorations. See page 18 for details.

C-8.

Felt and mirror ornaments add sparkle to Christmas trees. These can be made in a matter of minutes. See page 58 for details.

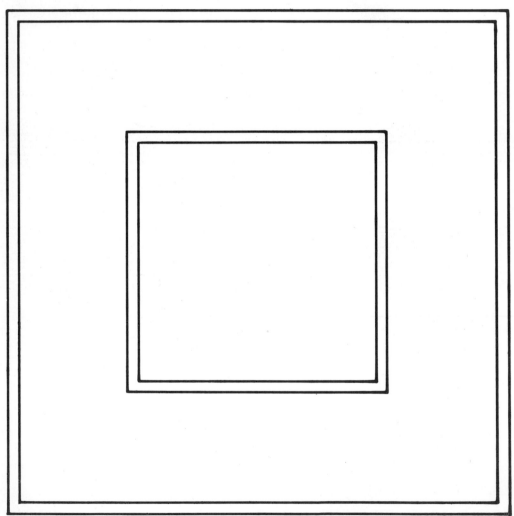

Inner Letter = 5″
Outer Letter = 5¼″

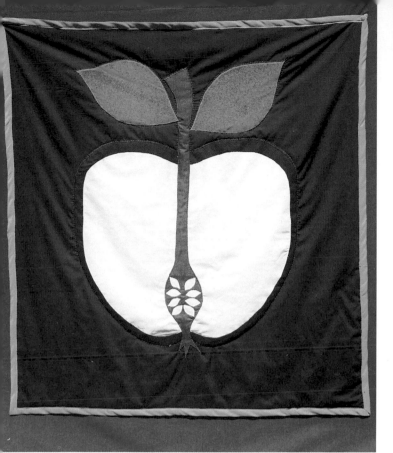

C-1

C-2

C-3

C-4

C-5   C-6   C-7   C-8

C-9

C-12

C-10

C-11

C-13

C-14

C-15

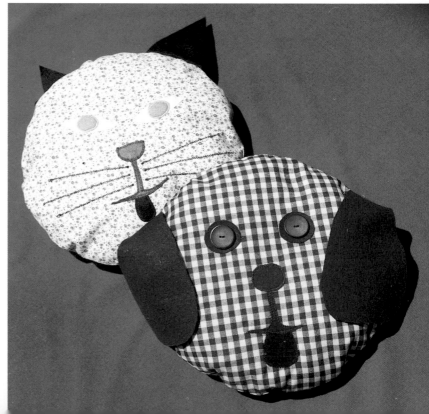

C-16

C-9.
Cross-stitch pictures are always popular items, and cross-stitch is adaptable to any number of designs for differing tastes. See page 67.

C-10.
The Three Wise Men are made of empty yarn cones, which can be obtained from needlework stores or departments. See page 21 for more details.

C-11.
These dried flower pictures are sure to go quickly at the bazaar. See page 93 for instructions.

C-12.
Vinyl is especially suitable for bibs or work aprons because it can be wiped clean with a damp cloth. The other bib shown is made with prequilted fabric. See details on page 128.

C-13.
A felt stocking, weed ornament, and stuffed snowman are simple Christmas ornaments to make. See pages 37, 56, and 59 for instructions.

C-14.
This roller skate stocking makes an interesting Christmas stocking for the shopper who wants something new and different. See instructions on page 24.

C-15.
These colorful finger puppets are made of beads and bits of fabric. See page 108 for details.

C-16.
The calico cat and gingham dog are pillows for a child's room. They're easy to make and are sure to be best sellers at the bazaar. Details are on page 120.

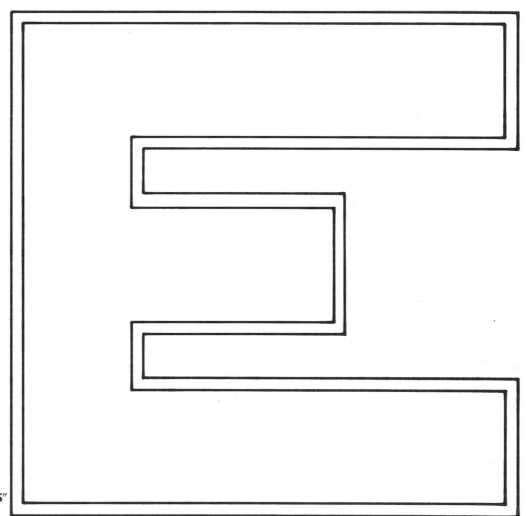

Inner Letter = 5″
Outer Letter = 5¼″

33

By using the alphabet on pages 136 through 139 you can spell out any number of messages for your fabric wall hangings.

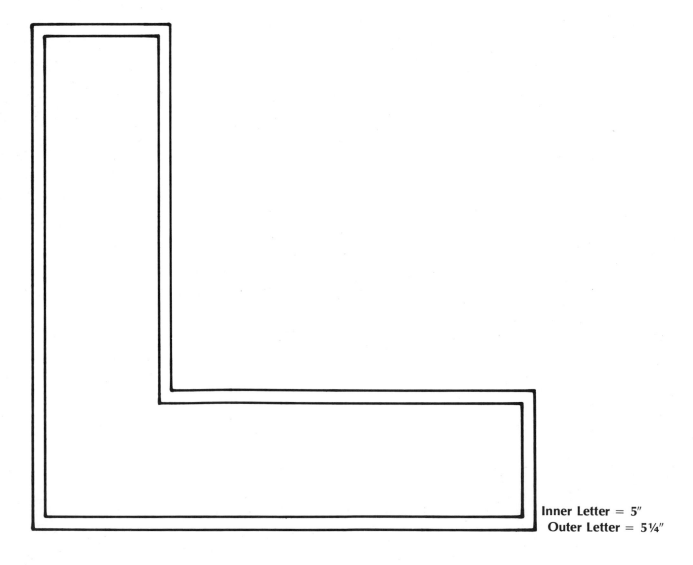

Inner Letter = 5″
Outer Letter = 5¼″

Sturdy fabric boards (the cores for bolts of fabric), make an ideal base on which to construct wall hangings. These boards are usually available free from fabric stores or departments. To begin making the hanging cover the board surface with white glue. A little water added to the glue will thin it so that it can be brushed on easily. Lay the fabric over the glued area and smooth out evenly. Glue the fabric to the sides and the back of the board. When dry, glue on a felt tree shape, cut as shown in the pattern, and decorate with sequins and ornaments cut from felt and ribbon.

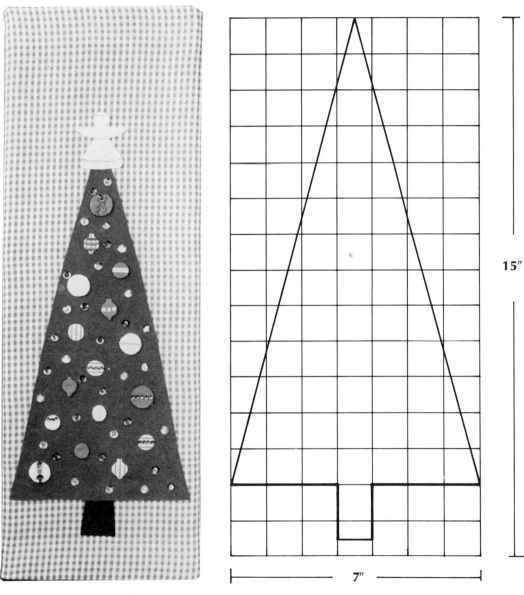

15"

7"

<u>Scale:</u> 1 square = 1 inch

35

Crocheted Snowman

This lovable snowman can be used for Christmas decorating or would make a delightful stocking stuffer for a small child. The following materials are enough for one snowman, measuring about 6 inches in height.

MATERIALS

white 3-ply yarn, 4 ounces
crochet hook, size F
thread
needle
Dacron batting
dark blue 3-ply yarn, 4 ounces
small pieces of red and dark blue felt
(*alternative:* sequins, ribbons, buttons)

DIRECTIONS

1. Make the snowman's head, using white yarn as follows:
   Row 1: Chain 3, close ring.
   Row 2: Chain 1, make 6 single crochets in ring, 1 single crochet in chain 1.
   Row 3: Chain 1, make 2 single crochets in each single crochet in previous ring, single crochet in chain 1.
   Row 4: Chain 1, * make 2 single crochets in first single crochet in previous row, 1 single crochet in next single crochet, repeat from * to end of row, 1 single crochet stitch in chain 1 (18 stitches).
   Row 5: Chain 1, * make 1 single crochet stitch in first stitch, 2 single crochets in second stitch, 1 single crochet in third stitch, repeat from * to end of row, 1 single crochet in chain 1 (24 stitches).
   Row 6: Repeat Row 4.
   Rows 7, 8, and 9: Make 1 single crochet stitch in each previous single crochet stitch.

   Make two pieces following the above directions. Stuff with Dacron batting and stitch the two sections together to form a ball.

2. Make the body as follows:
   Rows 1–6: Repeat Rows 1–6 of head.
   Row 7: Chain 1, * make 1 single crochet in each of the first 4 stitches, then 2 single crochets in fifth stitch, repeat from * to end of row.
   Rows 8–11: Chain 1, make 1 single crochet in each single crochet stitch.
   Make two pieces following the above directions. Stuff with Dacron batting and stitch together to form a ball.

3. Join head and body. Cut facial details from the felt and sew them on. Sequins, ribbon, or buttons could be used in place of felt for the features.

4. Make the snowman's hat as follows:
   Row 1: Chain 3, close ring.
   Row 2: Chain 1, make 6 single crochets in ring, close ring.
   Row 3: Chain 1, make 2 single crochets in each single crochet in previous ring, close ring.
   Row 4: Chain 1, * make 1 single crochet in first single crochet, 2 single crochets in next single crochet, repeat from * to end of row, close ring.
   Row 5: Repeat Row 3.
   Row 6: Chain 1, make 1 single crochet in each single crochet, draw tightly.
   Rows 7 and 8: Repeat Row 5.
   Row 9: Repeat Row 2.
   Row 10: Repeat Row 3.
   Shape hat and attach to head.

Straw Ornaments

Charming and unusual Christmas ornaments are always in demand and many of these can be made easily and inexpensively. Straw ornaments are inexpensive and easy to make. Long-stemmed weeds—wild wheat is especially good—should be gathered in late spring or early summer. (If the stalks are jointed, they should be separated at these joints.) Lay the sections out to dry. When the stems are dry and golden brown, they are ready to use; or they can be stored for later use.

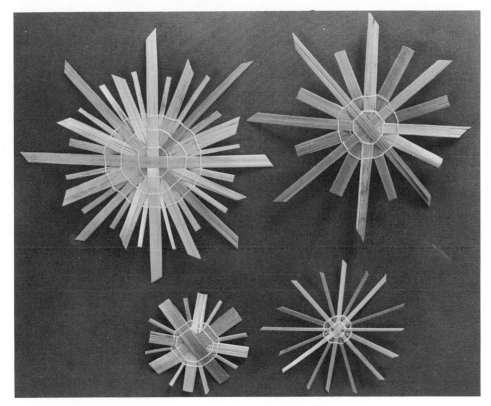

MATERIALS
weed stems, dried and golden brown
large, flat pan
iron
single-edged razor blade
scissors
thread

DIRECTIONS
1. Before the ornaments can be made, the stalks must first be softened. Lay the dried stems in a flat pan and cover with warm water. Allow them to soak overnight.
2. When soft, the stalks can be pressed flat with a warm iron. For wide pieces of straw, slit the larger stems with a single-edged razor blade and then press them open. The pressed straw can be cut into various lengths for different size ornaments.
3. All of the ornaments are done in multiples of four straws. Each unit of four straws should be bound together using thread, as shown.
4. Wrap the thread around the straws in this manner two times. Then reverse the direction, as shown. Go around twice and knot the ends on the back side.
5. Each four-straw unit produces an eight-point design. For a sixteen-point design, use two units and bind the two units together, as shown, going around twice, then reversing the direction and going around twice again.
6. Add a loop of thread on the back side for hanging.

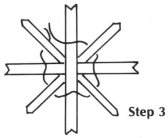

Step 3

Step 4

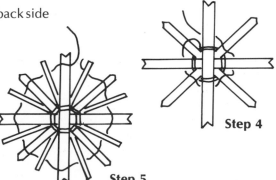

Step 5

Folded Paper Stars

Truly distinctive ornaments are these folded stars, which were popular tree decorations with the early Americans who made them from paper. Modern products, such as starched fabric ribbon and reversible wrapping paper, are ideal materials for making these stars.

MATERIALS
reversible wrapping paper
scissors
ruler
thread

DIRECTIONS
1. Cut four strips of paper, 17 inches in length and ⅝ inch wide.
2. Fold each strip of paper in half and position one within the other so that the strips are interlocking, as shown. Cut the ends of the strips to a point.

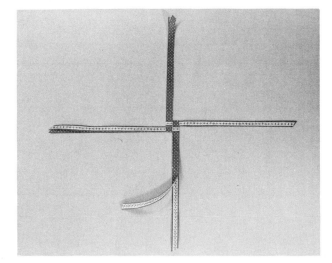

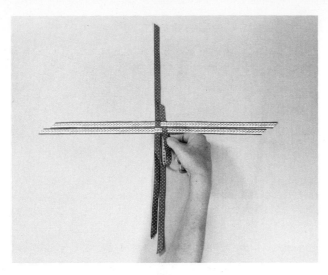

3. Fold the top strip of the left, over the interlocking section to the right. Next, fold the strip from the top downward. Then fold the left strip to the right. Take the bottom strip, fold upward, and insert under the fold of the first strip you folded, as shown. Pull into place. This creates an interlocking center as before with eight separate strips instead of four double ones.

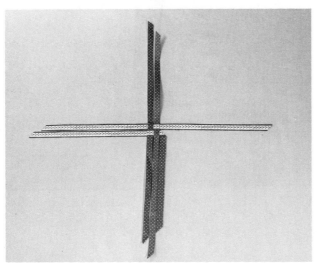

4. Starting with the lower strip on the right arm, fold under and down, as shown.

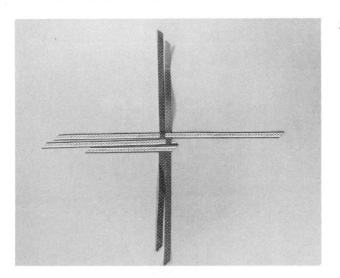

5. With that same strip, fold up and over to the left, point, as shown.

6. Fold the point in half, as shown.

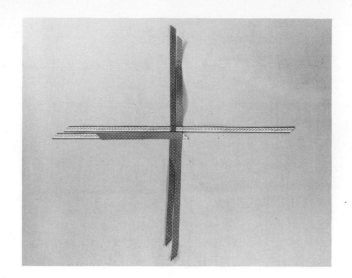

7. Picking up the work, bend the previously made point downward and slip the end of the strip under the fold of the nearest strip, as shown.

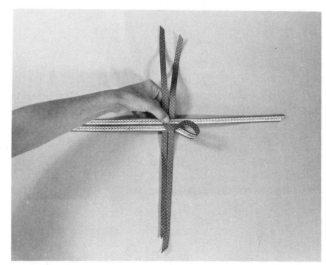

8. Pull gently into place, as shown.

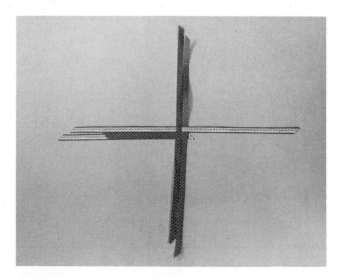

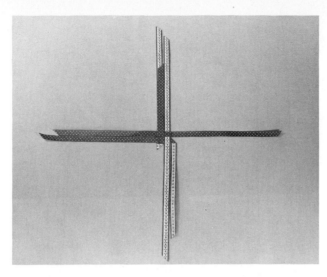

9. Rotate the work ¼ turn clockwise and repeat Step 4, as shown. Repeat steps 5–8 then repeat for remaining two sides.

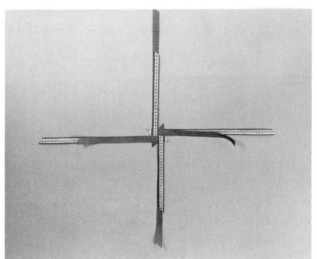

10. Four of the outer points are now complete, as shown. Turn the work upside down and repeat from Step 4.

11. There should now be eight outer points, as shown.

12. To begin making the three-dimensional center points pick up the work, lift the lower strip of the right arm upward. Take the lower strip of the left arm, bring around counter-clockwise, as shown, and slip the point under the strip which is being held upward.

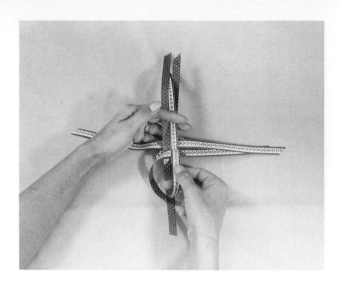

13. Push the strip through until the end comes out the star point above, as shown.

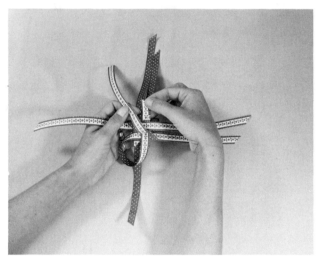

14. Pull the strip until a cone forms, as shown.

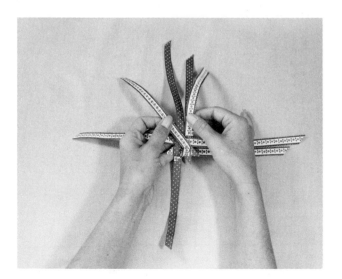

15. Turn the work ¼ to the left and repeat from Step 4 for each of the three remaining strips.

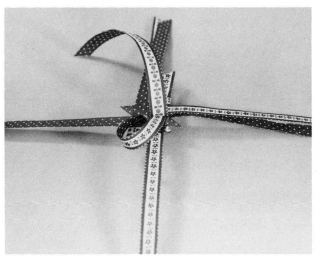

16. Turn the star over and repeat from Step 12.

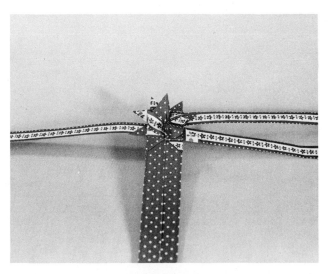

17. Trim ends of strips even with star points. Add a loop of thread for hanging.

Macaroni Ornaments

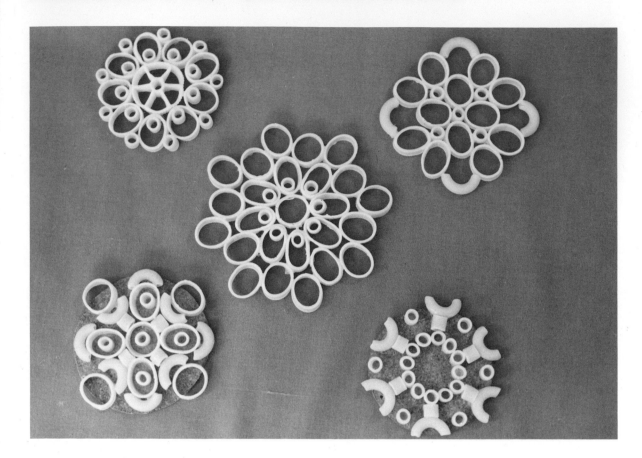

Macaroni can be used to make some lovely, lacy decorations. The photograph shows the use of several varieties of macaroni and noodle rings. Many other shapes are available and you may wish to include some of these. These ornaments are constructed on waxed paper which can easily be removed after the ornaments are dry. The procedure is very simple. You simply pour a small amount of white glue onto the waxed paper, dip the edges of the macaroni into the glue, and form your design. For those who feel they are "all thumbs," a tweezer can be used for handling the macaroni pieces.

Tin Can Angels

These dainty angels are made from tin can lids. Use the yellow side of the can lid for the front of the angel. For variety you may wish to paint some of the lids with white enamel and decorate with white lace or sections from a paper doily.

MATERIALS
tin can lid
tin snips
2 pairs of long-nosed pliers
bead
acrylic paint or model airplane enamel
fine brush, #0 or 00
white glue
gold trim or braid
yellow felt
gold thread

DIRECTIONS
1. Cut the lid, using tin snips, following the solid lines on the pattern.
2. Using two pairs of long-nosed pliers, bend along the dotted lines as follows: bend Line 1 up, bend Lines 2, 3, and 4 down, and bend Line 5 up. This will form the skirt and wings of the angel.
3. Bend Sections A and B forward slightly to form the arms.
4. Paint facial features on the bead. Glue the bead onto Section C.
5. Bend Section C so the head is inclined in the proper position.
6. Glue gold trim or braid around the edge of the skirt and wings.
7. Glue a small circle of yellow felt on the top of the bead head for hair. Add gold trim or braid around the felt piece to form the halo.
8. Tie a length of gold thread around Section C for hanging.

Cut on Solid Lines

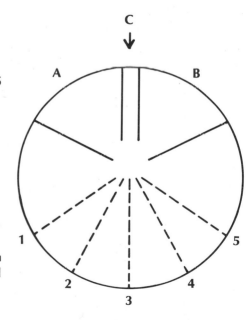

Bend on Dotted Lines

45

Plexiglas Ornaments

Those who've had experience with a jigsaw might want to try making some ornaments out of Plexiglas. These Plexiglas designs can be used as Christmas tree or gift package decorations. They could also be hung in a window for a bright spot of color.

A word about Plexiglas: Once you have become acquainted with its versatility, you might find more projects to do than there is time in which to do them. For most of these projects it is advisable to purchase scrap Plexiglas. This is generally sold by the pound, which is a much cheaper way to purchase than by buying premeasured sizes. Plexiglas comes with either a clear or paper covering to protect the surface from scratches. Do not remove. This covering should not be removed until after the design has been cut out.

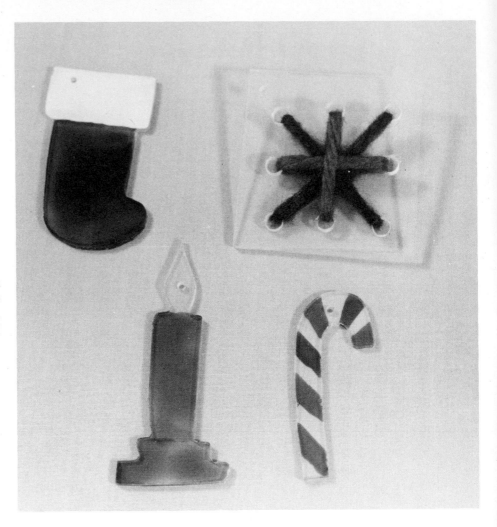

MATERIALS
Plexiglas
felt-tipped pen
jigsaw with a fine-tooth blade
drill
1/16-inch drill bit
glass stain
eyedropper
fishing line

DIRECTIONS

1. Use the patterns given here as templates and draw the designs on the Plexiglas, covering with a felt-tipped pen.
2. Cut the ornaments out using a jig-saw.
3. Drill $1/16$-inch holes at the top of each for hanging.
4. Remove the paper covering of the Plexiglas and paint with glass stain. An eyedropper is the ideal way to apply the stain, as it dries so rapidly.
5. Insert a length of fishing line through the drilled hole for hanging.

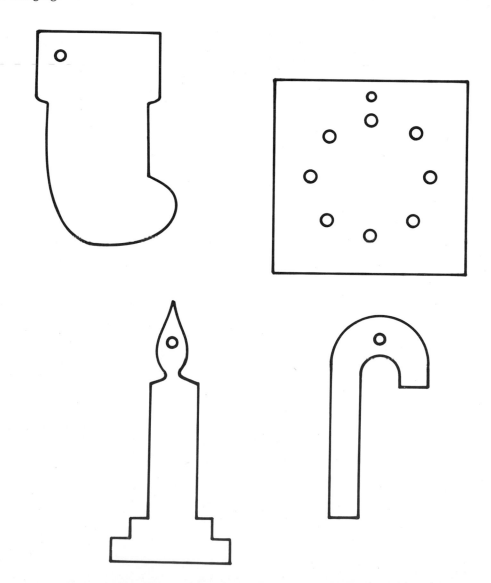

Bird's Nest Ornament

According to an old legend, peace and good fortune come to those who find a Christmas tree with a bird's nest in its branches. A charming bird's nest ornament would be a welcome addition to any holiday tree.

MATERIALS
excelsior
small juice glass
scissors
hair spray or lacquer
white glue
small pinch-type hair clip
small feathered or plastic bird (can be purchased in dime stores)
narrow ribbon
Optional: small white or pearl beads
Optional: a written copy of the bird's nest legend

DIRECTIONS
1. Soak the excelsior in warm water until soft. This will take fifteen to thirty minutes.
2. Remove a portion of excelsior from the water. Form a nest in the bottom of a juice glass with the excelsior and let it dry.
3. Remove the nest from the glass and trim away any loose ends with scissors.
4. Spray the nest with hair spray or lacquer to help bind the excelsior.
5. Glue a small pinch-type hair clip to the bottom of the nest. This clip will attach the nest to the tree branch.
6. Position the bird in the nest and glue in place.
7. A few small beads may be added to represent eggs if desired, or purchase baby birds from dime store.
8. Glue a small colorful bow to the front of the nest.
9. If you wish, attach a copy of the legend with the hair clip.

Rudolf Tree Ornament

Rudolf is always a favorite Christmas character. This soft, fluffy Rudolf would make a charming tree ornament, but he could also be used as a delightful package decoration or stocking stuffer.

MATERIALS
brown yarn pom-pom, 1 inch in diameter for each
brown yarn pom-pom, 1½ inches in diameter for each
white glue
scissors
brown felt
jiggly eyes
red felt
brown yarn

DIRECTIONS
1. Securely glue the small pom-pom onto the larger one.
2. Trim the sides of the small pom-pom to shape the nose.
3. Cut antlers from brown felt, using the pattern given, and glue in place.
4. Add jiggly eyes and a red felt dot for the nose.
5. Add a length of yarn for hanging.

White Glue Ornaments

Truly unique ornaments can be made using white glue as the primary ingredient. When the white glue dries it provides a translucent background that enhances the delicate designs in the ornament.

MATERIALS
plastic lid
white glue
whole cloves
whole peppercorns
mustard seeds
needle
thread

DIRECTIONS
1. Fill the center depression on the top of the plastic lid with white glue.
2. Arrange cloves, peppercorns, and mustard seeds.
3. Let dry until the glue is hard and translucent. Be patient—this may take about three days.
4. Carefully peel away the plastic lid.
5. Make a hole at the top with a needle and add a thread for hanging.

You may wish to experiment with other types of materials for making the design, such as tiny metal washers, sequins, small macaroni pieces or beads.

The other ornament shown in the picture was done without using a plastic lid mold. This type of ornament is made on a sheet of cardboard which has been covered with waxed paper. The gold metallic cord is pinned into the desired shape, and the glue is then poured inside. Here tiny dried flowers were used to create the delicate design. After drying, the waxed paper can be peeled away and a ribbon glued on the back for hanging.

Stamp Ornaments

These are two simple ornaments that can be made by children who wish to participate in the bazaar preparations.

Simple, but attractive tokens of Christmases past and present are made from Christmas postage stamps. These could be new or cancelled postage stamps or even seasonal stamps from charitable organizations. Using colored posterboard for the background, a stamp is glued on each side. A thread is added for hanging. Some children also like to date the stamp with the year it was issued. This could even become a Christmas tradition: each year a new stamp ornament could be added to the collection.

A similar type of ornament can be made by simply applying adhesive-backed irridescent foil to squares of balsa wood. This type of foil comes in a variety of patterns and is most easily obtained from an art-supply store or plastics specialty shop. The balsa wood is cut to the desired size using an X-acto knife. Older children can do this themselves, but younger children should be assisted in cutting the balsa wood. The cut edges of the wood are colored with a permanent felt-tipped marker and the foil is applied to both sides. Finally, a thread hanger is added. The rainbow colors that occur as the ornament spins will add a sparkle to the Christmas tree.

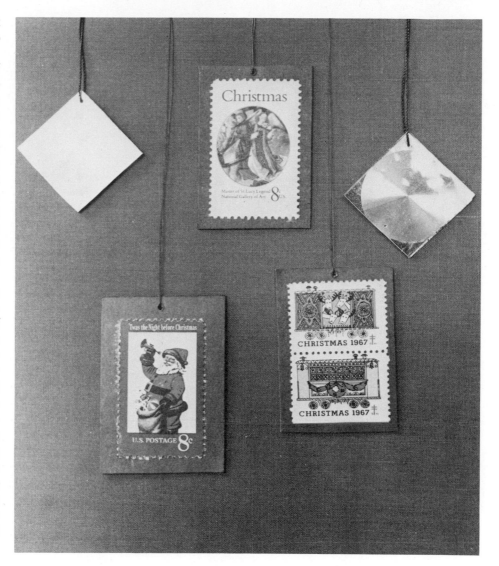

Crocheted Star, Wreath, and Bell Ornaments

Crocheted ornaments are very attractive and yet are quite simple to make. The wreath in the picture below was made by crocheting around a 1-inch-diameter plastic curtain ring using a 4-ounce skein of three-ply green yarn. Use a size G crochet hook and crochet around the ring, in single crochets, until the ring is completely covered. Then tie off. Attach tiny red beads for the holly berries, a small red bow, and a thread for hanging.

The lacy, delicate star and bell are made using crochet thread rather than yarn. Both of these ornaments will have to be starched in a sugar-water solution in order for them to hold their shape. The starching solution should be four parts of sugar to one part water. Heat the solution until all the sugar has dissolved; then dip the ornaments and secure in position for drying.

MATERIALS FOR STAR

white crochet thread, size 30, 4 yards
crochet hook, size 9
starching solution (4 parts sugar: 1 part water)
straight pins

DIRECTIONS

1. Crochet the star as follows:
   Row 1: Chain 10, close ring.
   Row 2: Chain 9, make 1 double crochet in ring. * Chain 6, double crochet in ring, repeat from * 3 times. Chain 6 and join to 3rd stitch in 1st chain (6 loops).
   Row 3: Slip stitch to 3rd stitch in 1st chain of previous row.
   Row 4: *Chain 10, make 1 double crochet in 3rd stitch from end, chain 3, slip stitch at bottom of double crochet, chain 7, and make 1 single crochet in next loop. Repeat from * 5 times. Tie off.
2. Dip star in starching solution, stretch out, and pin flat in star shape. Let dry.
3. Add thread hanger.

MATERIALS FOR BELL

white crochet thread, size 30, 21 yards
crochet hook, size 9
starching solution
paper drinking cup, 3-ounce size
straight pins
narrow ribbon
Styrofoam ball, ¾-inch diameter

DIRECTIONS

1. Crochet the bell as follows:
   Row 1: Chain 6, then close ring.
   Row 2: Chain 3, make 15 double crochets in ring. Close ring.
   Row 3: Chain 8, skip 2 double crochets, make 1 double crochet in space. * Chain 5, skip 2 double crochets, make 1 double crochet in space, repeat from * to end of row. Chain 5, join to 3rd stitch in the chain 8 (8 spaces).
   Row 4: Slip stitch to 2nd stitch in next chain of 5. Chain 3, make 1 double crochet in loop, chain 1, 2 double crochets in loop, chain 3. * Make 2 double crochets, chain 1, 2 double crochets in next loop. Chain 3, repeat from * to end of row. Join to top chain 3 of previous row.
   Row 5: Slip stitch to chain 1 of previous row. Chain 3, make 1 double crochet in chain-1 space, 2 double crochets, chain 3. * Make 2 double crochets in chain-1 space, chain 1, 2 double crochets in same space, chain 3, repeat from * to end of row. Join.

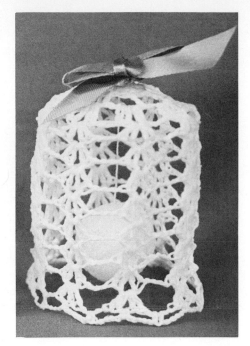

   Rows 6–10: Repeat Row 5.
   Row 11: Slip stitch to stitch-1 opening. * Chain 5, make 1 single crochet in 3-stitch opening, chain 5. Slip stitch in chain-1 opening, repeat from * to end of row.
2. Dip bell in starch solution and form over the drinking cup, pinning as necessary to hold the shape. Let dry.
3. Insert a length of crochet thread through the Styrofoam ball and attach at the top of the bell. This represents the clapper of the bell.
4. Attach a tiny ribbon bow and a thread for hanging.

Knitted Bird Ornament

Knitted ornaments can be interesting additions to a collection of tree decorations. The bird pictured could be made from any color yarn desired, but red and white would be most appropriate for a tree decoration. Since the bird is stuffed with Dacron batting, it could be a soft toy to tuck into youngster's Christmas stocking. The materials given here are for eight birds.

MATERIALS

red 3-ply yarn, 4 ounces
skein white 3-ply yarn, 4 ounces
knitting needles, size 5
large needle
Dacron batting
16 sequins

DIRECTIONS

1. Cast on 8 stitches with red yarn and knit the bird as follows:
   Row 1: Knit 8.
   Row 2: Purl across.
   Row 3: Knit 1, increase in 2nd stitch, knit 4, increase in next stitch, knit 1.
   Row 4: Purl across.
   Row 5, 7, 9, 11, 13, 15, and 17: Repeat Row 3.
   Rows 6, 8, 10, 12, 14, 16, and 18: Purl across.
   Row 19: Knit across.
   Row 20: Purl across.
   Row 21: Knit 1, knit 2 together twice. Knit to within 5 stitches of end. Knit 2 together twice, knit 1.
   Row 22: Purl across.
   Row 23: Bind off 2 stitches, knit remainder of row.
   Row 24: Bind off 2 stitches, purl remainder of row.
   Row 25: Repeat Row 23.
   Row 26: Repeat Row 24.
   Row 27: Bind off 1 stitch, knit across, alternating red and white yarn.
   Row 28: Bind off 1 stitch, purl across, alternating red and white yarn.
   Row 29: Repeat Row 27.
   Row 30: Repeat Row 28.
   Row 31: With white yarn, knit 2 together, knit to within last 2 stitches, knit 2 together.
   Row 32: Purl across.
   Row 33: Knit across.
   Row 34: Purl across.
   Row 35: Knit across.
   Row 36: Purl across.
   Row 37: Knit across alternately with red and white.
   Row 38: Purl across with red.
   Row 39: Knit 2 together, knit to within last 2 stitches, knit 2 together.
   Row 40: Purl across.
   Row 41: Bind off.
2. Stitch the edges together, leaving an opening for stuffing. Fill with Dacron batting and stitch closed.
3. Attach sequins for eyes and yarn for hanging.

Knitted Bell and Stocking Ornaments

Two more knitted Christmas decorations that can be used either on a tree or as a package tie are a bell and stocking. These ornaments are especially charming, as the bell really jingles and the stocking can hold wrapped Christmas candy. The materials given here are enough for four bells and seven stockings.

MATERIALS FOR BELL
red 3-ply yarn, 2 ounces
knitting needles, size 4
4 jingle bells
large needle

DIRECTIONS
1. Cast on 16 stitches and knit the bell as follows:
   Row 1: Knit across.
   Row 2: Purl 4, knit 12.
   Rows 3–46: Repeat Rows 1 and 2.
   Row 47: Bind off.
2. Stitch up the side seam, and gather top tightly to form bell.
3. To finish the bell attach a jingle bell to a length of yarn and stitch yarn to the inside top of the bell. Attach another piece of yarn for hanging.

MATERIALS FOR STOCKING
white 3-ply yarn, 2 ounces
knitting needles, size 4
red 3-ply yarn, 2 ounces
needle

DIRECTIONS
1. Cast on 20 stitches, using white yarn, and knit stocking as follows:
   Rows 1–7: Knit 1, purl 1 to end of row. After 7th row change to red yarn.
   Rows 8–13: Work in stockinette stitch (knit and purl on alternate rows).
   Row 14: Knit 1, knit 2 together, knit 4, increase in next 4 stitches, knit 7, knit 2 together, knit 1.
   Rows 18–21: Work in stockinette stitch.
   Row 22: Bind off.
2. Sew edges together, leaving two strands of yarn for hanging.

55

Stocking and Skate Ornaments

A small stocking or a pair of skates made from felt would make delightful party favors. The patterns provided for these perky little ornaments are the actual size used for cutting.

MATERIALS FOR STOCKING
red felt
scissors
straight pins
lace trim
sewing machine

DIRECTIONS
1. Cut two pieces of felt, using the pattern.
2. Pin lace and hanging loop in place.
3. Machine-stitch around edge of stocking, and tuck in a Christmas treat.

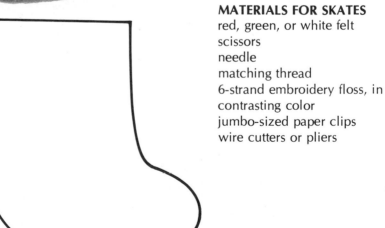

MATERIALS FOR SKATES
red, green, or white felt
scissors
needle
matching thread
6-strand embroidery floss, in contrasting color
jumbo-sized paper clips
wire cutters or pliers

DIRECTIONS

1. Place pattern on felt fold, as shown by dotted lines. Cut two of these for a pair of skates.
2. Sew the sides closed with a whipstitch, using thread the same color as the felt.
3. "Lace" the skates with a length of six-strand embroidery floss in a color contrasting to the color of the felt. Tie the ends in a bow.
4. The skate blades are jumbo-sized paper clips, snipped as shown. Use either wire cutters or pliers to cut the clips.
5. Insert the paper clip through the skate just above the fold.
6. A length of thread or embroidery floss can be used to hang the skates.

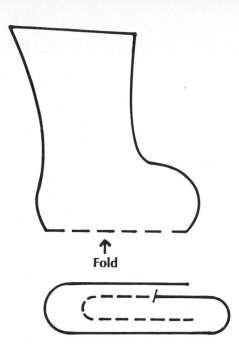

Fold

The roller skates are assembled in the same manner as the ice skates. The wheels, which are small beads, are stitched through offset holes to the bottom edge of the skate.

Felt and Mirror Ornaments

These brightly colored felt and mirror ornaments bring additional sparkle to the holiday season. These tiny mirrors are available in hobby shops in a variety of sizes and shapes. Cut two pieces of felt ½ inch larger than the mirror. Cut a window in one of the felt pieces to expose the center portion of the mirror. At this point, attach any decorative shapes desired to the felt back. Then place the mirror between the two pieces of felt and machine-stitch around the edge of the mirror. Add a thread for hanging. For variation, try having mirrors peeking out of both sides of the ornament. A group of these could be combined to form a truly unique holiday mobile.

Stuffed Snowmen

White felt can be used to create some saucy snowmen. Bright calico adds a cheerful note to these cute little stuffed ornaments.

MATERIALS
white felt
scissors
sequins and beads
needle
thread
Dacron batting
small pices of calico

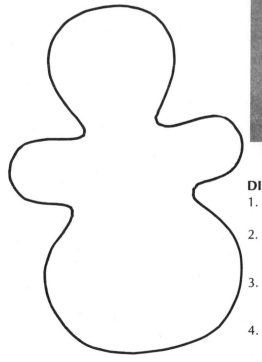

DIRECTIONS

1. Cut two pieces of felt using the pattern given.
2. Stitch on black beads and/or sequins for eyes and nose. Add the mouth, using an outline stitch.
3. Sew beads and sequins in place for buttons. These should complement the color of the calico being used.
4. Whipstitch around the edge of the snowman. Before stitching is completed, stuff the figure with Dacron batting and then complete stitching.
5. Add a calico scarf and a cone-shaped hat. Stitch the hat in place.
6. A small ball of batting glued to the top of the hat completes the snowman.
7. Add a thread for hanging.

Nutshell Ornaments

The use of natural materials provides a nice change of pace in the making of tree ornaments. Nuts, because of their shapes, are particularly adaptable for this use. Although examples here show hazelnut, almond, and walnut shells, you may wish to experiment with other varieties, such as peanuts, chestnuts, and pecans.

In the pictures here the nuts are used to provide the bodies for the figures. A small bead, on which a face has been painted, is glued in place for the head. It is best to use either acrylic paint or model airplane enamel, applied with a very fine brush (#0 or #00), to paint the tiny features.

To complete the hazelnut elf add a cone-shaped hat of felt with just a wisp of hair tucked under the front edge and glued in place. The hair can be either frayed jute or yarn. A yarn hatband and tiny feather added to the hat give the elf a jaunty air.

Hair and wings are needed to complete the almond angel. Hair may be made from dried coffee grounds, cornmeal, or felt. The hair area is painted with white glue and then the desired type of hair is applied. Wings are cut from silver posterboard (available at art-supply stores) and are glued on the back of the angel.

60

Decorated walnut shell halves add a whimsical note to holiday decorating. The comical faces peering out from under the red felt hats of the Santa Mice have jiggly eyes, string whiskers, and tiny bead noses. The hat is a cone shape, the top of which is folded over, and a ball of Dacron batting is attached to the end. Yarn or string should be added for the tail. A toothpick can be used to aid in gluing these small decorations in place. Sew a thread through the top of the hat for a hanger.

A walnut shell half can also serve as a cradle for a tiny bead baby. First, glue the ribbon hanger inside the upper edge of the walnut shell and then stuff the cradle with Dacron batting. Facial features should be painted on a small bead and embroidery floss can be glued on for the hair. Then the head is glued in place in the cradle and a tiny calico blanket tucked in up to the "chin."

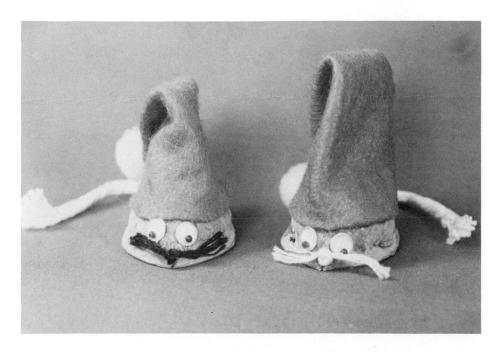

Little Bead Cherubs

Dainty cherubs make a nice addition to a nativity scene or could be combined with other small ornaments to form a holiday mobile. The natural tones of the wooden beads give each cherub an individual character.

MATERIALS

round wooden beads
acrylic paint or model airplane enamel
fine brush, #0 or 00
glue
dried coffee grounds or saw dust
golf tees or bell-shaped wooden beads
pruning shears
strip of wood veneer or posterboard

DIRECTIONS

1. Paint faces on the wooden beads, using a fine brush.
2. Glue dried coffee grounds or saw dust onto a portion of the head for hair.
3. The body of the cherub can be a bell-shaped bead or a golf tee. If the golf tee is used, clip off a portion of the pointed end with pruning shears. Glue the head and body together.
4. Cut triangular-shaped wings from wood veneer or posterboard, and glue in place.

3 Gifts Galore

In addition to Christmas decorations and ornaments a nice variety of hand-made gifts are an important part of any bazaar offering. Gift giving is not limited to the holiday season, and, therefore, the gift selection should be suitable for other occasions. Some projects would make elegant birthday gifts, such as an afghan or a cut-paper picture, while a dried flower arrangement, key chain, or cookbook would make a perfect hostess or thank you gift.

Cut Paper Designs

A truly elegant picture can be made from such simple items as white typing paper and a pair of sharp scissors. A symmetrical design results from folding the paper in half and cutting the picture. The experience is similar to cutting valentine hearts or paper dolls, except that in this case the design is more detailed. The photographs on page 66 show that simple and very intricate pictures can be produced by this method. Start with a simple idea and then, as you gain experience, attempt more difficult designs.

MATERIALS

1 sheet of typing paper, 8½ by 11 inches
small, sharp scissors
pencil

DIRECTIONS

1. Fold a sheet of typing paper in half, making a sharp crease at the center.
2. Begin cutting the outer edge of the design. Use the design given here or come up with your own. It may be helpful to lightly sketch the design in pencil first, to aid in the cutting.
3. Cut the inside area of the design.

Remember that, when working with a design other than the one given here, if you cut through the center crease the design must be attached to the outside edge somewhere else. Otherwise, you will have 2 separate designs.

4. After the cutting is completed, carefully pull apart the two sides of the design.

Dotted Line Indicates Fold

Cut paper designs are even more lovely when framed. The intricately cut pictures are greatly enhanced by mounting them on a background of delicately patterned fabric before framing.

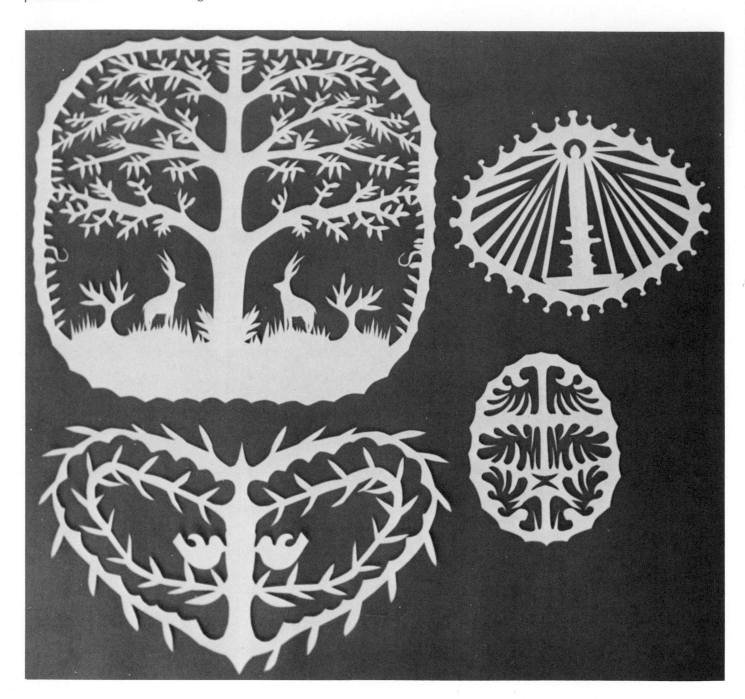

Cross-Stitch Pictures

A small cross-stitch picture can be framed for charming wall decorations. Waffle-weave pique or birdseye material is ideal for cross-stitch because the fabric already has a square texture. You will need the following materials to make one picture.

MATERIALS

waffle-weave pique or birdseye, 6 by 6 inches
embroidery hoop, 5-inch
embroidery needle
dark orange 2-strand embroidery floss
light orange 2-strand embroidery floss
yellow 2-strand embroidery floss
green 2-strand embroidery floss
scissors
wooden ring, 3¼ inches in diameter
white glue
white felt
compass
brass picture hanger

DIRECTIONS

1. Place fabric in embroidery hoop and begin cross-stitching the design, following the pattern.
2. After the design is completed, apply glue to the back of the wooden ring. Place the ring over the fabric centering the design in the ring and press down.
3. After the glue has dried, trim away the excess fabric.
4. Draw a 3-inch circle on white felt and cut it out. Glue the circle on the back of the picture.
5. Attach brass picture hanger.

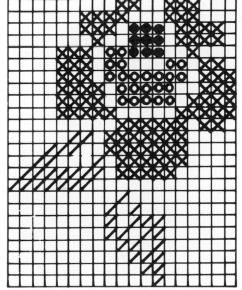

● = **Dark Orange**

○ = **Light Orange**

/ = **Green**

X = **Yellow**

Other designs can be adapted for these kinds of pictures by using graph paper, each square on the paper corresponding to a square on the fabric, and graph paper has been provided in the back of the book for this purpose. Using one cross-stitch per square, transfer the design from the graph paper to the fabric with two strands of embroidery floss. Patterns could be adapted from other cross-stitch, latch hook, or needlepoint designs. The finished picture can then be framed, using either small picture frames or wooden curtain rings.

Follow the directions on page 67 to make any of these cross-stitch projects.

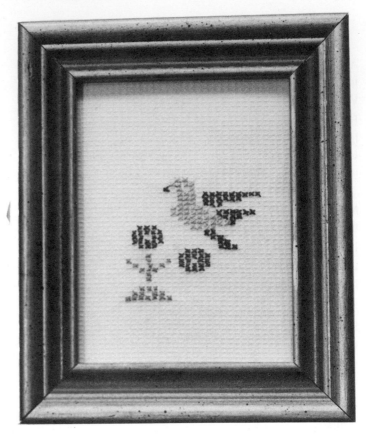

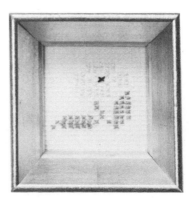

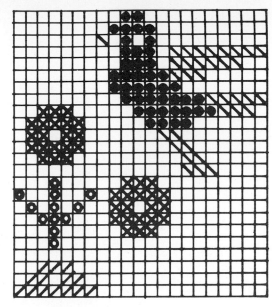

● = Light Blue

○ = Light Green

/ = Dark Green

x = Purple

\ = Dark Blue

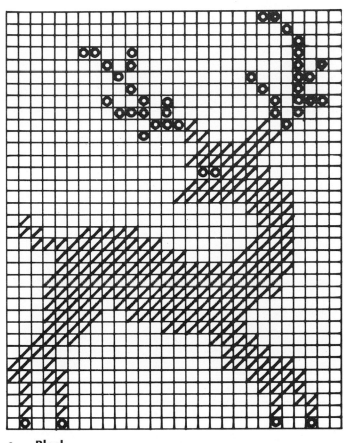

○ = Black

/ = Brown

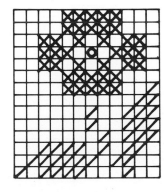

○ = Brown

x = Yellow

/ = Green

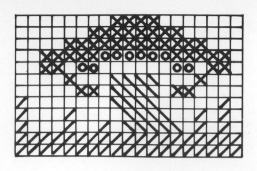

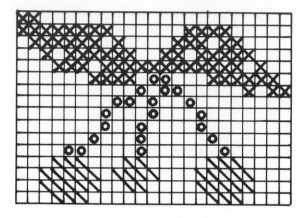

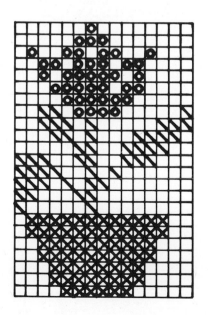

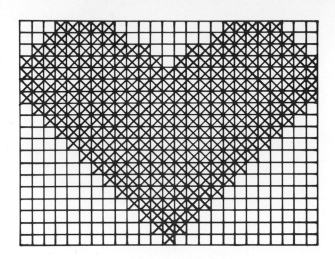

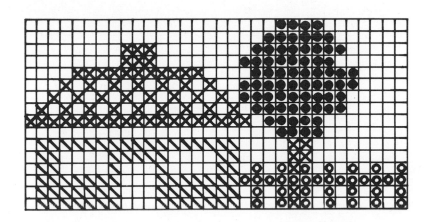

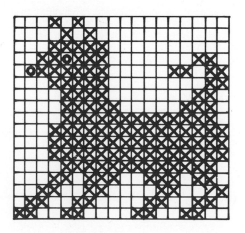

Felt Appliqué Pictures

The art of felt appliqué can be used to create some colorful designs. The design itself is made up of brightly colored pieces of felt which are appliquéd on a selected background. The pieces are appliquéd in place using a running stitch or French knots. In the pictures shown small pieces of felt and burlap were used as the backgrounds. Patterns for the flower and mushroom design are given here.

The least expensive way of providing a wide color selection for the felt appliqué is to purchase precut felt squares. In this way, it is possible to obtain colors not usually available by the yard.

An unusual, but simple, method of framing felt pictures is to use small embroidery hoops. Simply center the design, place it in the hoop, trim away excess material, and attach a brass hanger.

Quilted Pictures

Small quilted pictures are particularly suitable for use as kitchen decorations. Because the pieces used in forming the pictures are quite small, this is an excellent way to use up fabric remnants. Calico, gingham, and other small print fabrics can be combined to form an attractive design. Directions are given here for the "Coffee Time" design and patterns for all three designs are also given.

MATERIALS

gingham yellow-and-white fabric, 9½ by 11 inches

brown-with-white-polka-dot fabric, 6 by 5 inches

green-with-white-polka-dot fabric, 3½ by 3 inches

brown fabric, 1 by 2 inches

scissors

fusible interfacing

iron

sewing machine

black or brown permanent felt-tipped marker

yellow fabric, 9½ by 11 inches

Dacron batting

needle

quilting thread to match fabrics

brown bias tape, 1½ yards

DIRECTIONS

1. Cut appliqué pieces, using the patterns. Cut the coffee pot from the brown-with-white-polka-dot fabric, the cup from the green-with-white-polka-dot fabric, and the "coffee" from the solid brown.

2. Cut fusible interfacing, using the same patterns. Place the interfacing between the appliqué pieces and the gingham background and press with a warm iron.

3. Using a zigzag stitch and matching thread, machine-appliqué around the edges of the pieces.

4. Draw in the letters and steam on the fabric, using the permanent felt-tipped marker.

5. Place a layer of Dacron batting between the picture and the yellow backing fabric and pin together.

6. Quilt around the coffee pot, the cup, and each word.

7. Cut two pieces of bias tape, each about 3 inches long. Fold each piece in half and pin in place on the back side of the hanging. Match the cut edges of the tape to the upper edge of the picture. These loops will be the hangers for the picture.

8. Bind all the edges of the picture with brown bias tape. After this is completed, fold up the hanging loops and tack to the bias tape edging.

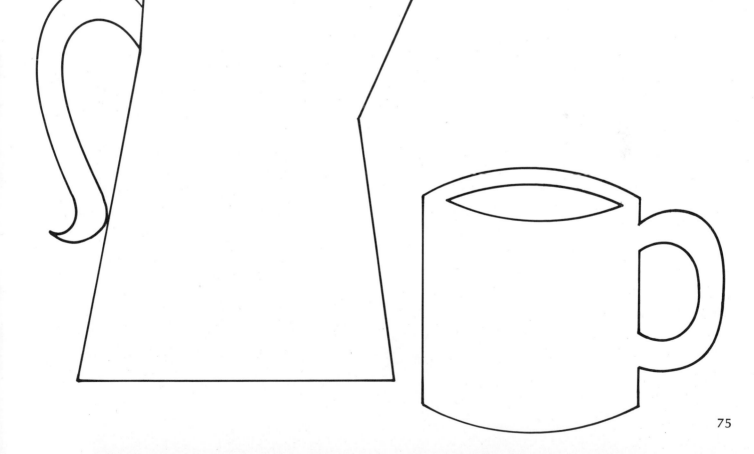

Scale: 1 square = 1 inch

76

Scale: 1 square = 1 inch

*Here are some additional designs for
quilted pictures.*

Scale: 1 square = 1 inch

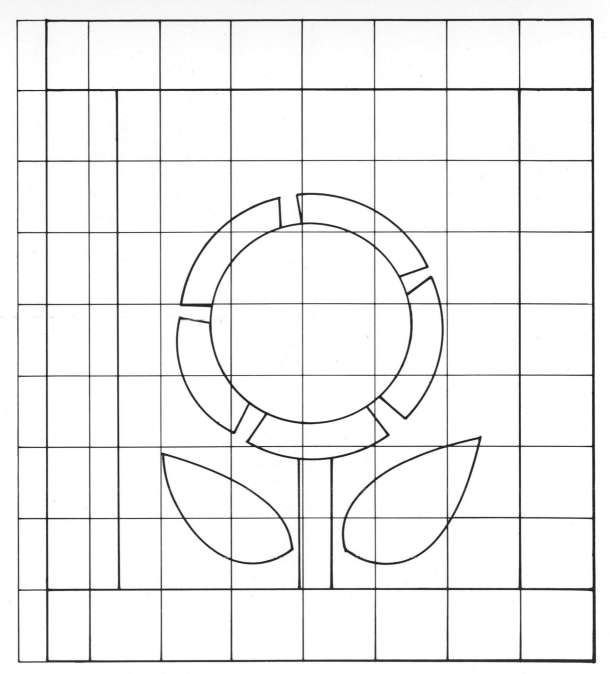

Scale: 1 square = 1 inch

Quilts and Afghans

Small quilts and afghans are always very popular at bazaars since they make such nice gifts. A very simple way of making a small quilt or lap robe is to utilize pre-quilted fabric for the quilt top. A soft cotton or flannel material can serve as the backing fabric. The front and back pieces can be bound together with extra-wide bias tape in a harmonizing color. By using some of the quilted prints designed for children, this method can be used to make some delightful baby quilts.

80

Appliquéd Afghan

An appliquéd afghan such as this provides an opportunity for the maker to express his creativity. A simple design can be used to produce striking results, with a minimum of time and effort.

MATERIALS

navy blue fabric, 44 by 48 inches
red fabric, 30 by 28 inches
white fabric, 28 by 25 inches
brown fabric, 6 by 38 inches
green fabric, 19 by 20 inches
yellow fabric, 5 by 5 inches
scissors
straight pins

sewing machine
backing fabric, 44 by 48 inches
Dacron batting
needle
quilting thread
apple green extra-wide bias tape, 16
 feet

DIRECTIONS

1. Using the patterns, cut the largest apple shape from the red fabric and the smaller one from the white. Cut a brown stem, two green leaves, and eight yellow seeds.
2. Place the red apple shape on the background piece so that the lowest part of the apple is about 8½ inches from the bottom edge of the background. Allow about 8 inches on each side. Pin in place and machine-appliqué using a zigzag stitch.
3. Place the white apple shape on top of the red one and stitch.
4. Appliqué the stem, and then the leaves and seeds.
5. Assemble the appliquéd top, Dacron batting, and backing piece for quilting. Pin the layers together, starting in the center of the afghan and working toward the edges. Place the pins every 4 or 5 inches to ensure against shifting during quilting.
6. Quilt around the apple form, using quilting thread in a running stitch.
7. Bind the edges together with extra-wide bias tape.

Outer Apple

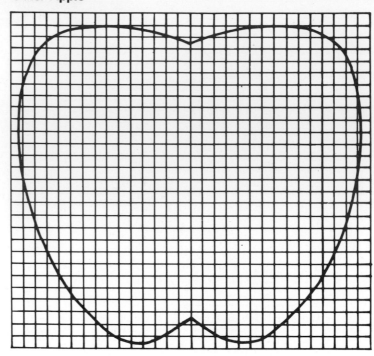

Core

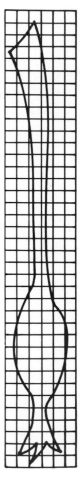

Leaf

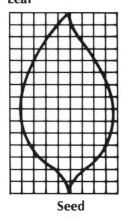

Seed

Inner Apple

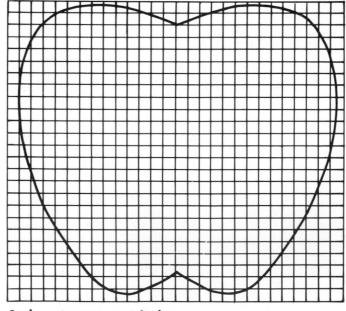

82

Scale: 1 square = 1 inch

Patchwork Coverlet

A good way to use up fabric remnants is to create a small patchwork coverlet. The one shown in the photograph is a good project for anyone not familiar with patchwork, as it requires only one 3-inch-square pattern piece. Those more experienced in this area may wish to use a more complicated design. The patchwork pieces may be arranged to produce a definite pattern or they may be randomly combined. This will be determined to some extent by the amount and color of remnants available.

To make a small coverlet like the one shown cut the fabric into 3-inch squares. This size allows for a ½-inch seam allowance on each side and thus will make a 2-inch square block when stitched. Using the 2-inch square block as a measurement, determine the number of pieces to be cut for the desired size coverlet. Stitch the patches together. Combine the finished top with a layer of Dacron batting and a backing, and pin the layers together. At this point, the little coverlet is ready to be quilted or tied. Finish by binding the edges.

Lacy Throw Pillow

Small throw pillows make ideal fabric projects for bazaar booths. The addition of an attractive design makes this a more appealing item. A lacy doily gives a throw pillow a delicate and nostalgic touch.

MATERIALS

cover background fabric, 13 by 13 inches
doily, 9 or 10 inches in diameter
straight pins
needle
thread
backing fabric, 13 by 13 inches
sewing machine
scissors
square pillow form, 12 inches

DIRECTIONS

1. Center the doily on the cover fabric. Pin in place. Beginning about 1 inch from the center, tack the doily to the cover. Going in a circle, tack stitch every inch or so. Continue making these circles, about 1 inch apart, until the doily is well secured to the cover.
2. You may wish to add French knots in the centers of some of the open areas and around the outer edge of the doily to enhance the design.
3. Place the backing fabric on the cover, right sides together, and stitch around the edge leaving 9 or 10 inches open on one side for filling.
4. Trim corners and turn right side out.
5. Place pillow inside the cover and stitch the opening closed.

Rainbow Tote Bag

Tote bags are great items for bazaars. Not only are they popular gift items, but shoppers like to buy them at bazaars to hold their purchases. The basic bag can be quickly assembled using canvas fabric and can be decorated in a variety of ways. A rainbow is an especially colorful motif.

MATERIALS

2 pieces of canvas fabric, each 18 by 14 inches
bias tape in rainbow colors—violet, dark blue, bright blue, green, yellow, orange, and red
2 canvas strips, each 20 by 3 inches
sewing maching
straight pins

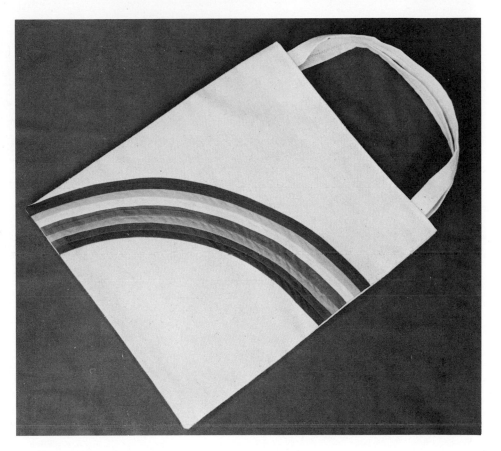

DIRECTIONS

1. Using one of the canvas pieces as the front, begin machine-stitching the bias tape in place. Overlap each color of tape over the edge of the preceding color to keep the colors solid and even.
2. The long narrow strips of canvas are used for the handles. Fold as shown in the diagram and top-stitch over the seam, using a zigzag stitch.
3. To finish the upper edges of the tote bag, fold 1½ inches to the inside. This allows a 1 inch (2.5 cm.) hem and a ½-inch seam allowance. Pin the ends of the handles under the hem and fold upward before stitching the hem.
4. With right sides together, stitch the remaining three sides closed using a ½-inch seam allowance.

Prequilted Placemats

Reversible quilted fabrics are available in a wide selection of patterns. Because the patterns on the two sides are different, the reversible fabric is particularly suitable for placemats. The following directions are for one placemat.

MATERIALS

reversible quilted fabric, 17 by 12 inches
scissors
bias tape, 5 feet
sewing machine
iron-on tape
iron

DIRECTIONS

1. Cut the placemat from the fabric, according to the pattern.
2. Bind the edges of cut fabric with bias tape.
3. Cut iron-on tape designs, using the patterns.
4. Iron the design onto the placemat.

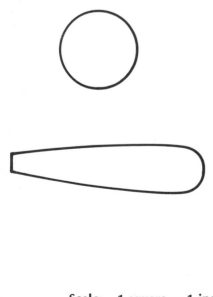

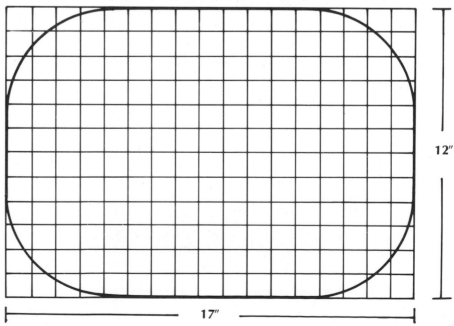

Scale: 1 square = 1 inch

12"

17"

Napkins and Napkin Rings

A set of coordinated napkins and napkin rings make a nice gift idea. Fabrics and designs can be used to make these sets, which are fitting for a particular holiday or special occasion. You might also wish to offer a selection of brightly colored napkins, which can be purchased singly or in a mix or match combination. Attractive napkin rings can be made from 1½-inch sections cut from heavy cardboard tubing. Colored decorator tape can be applied to the outside surface of the rings. The cut edges of the rings are colored with permanent felt-tipped markers to mask them. Decorate with gummed designs or ribbon. To make the napkins choose a fabric in a complementary pattern and cut in 14-inch squares. The edges of the napkins can be hemmed or fringed.

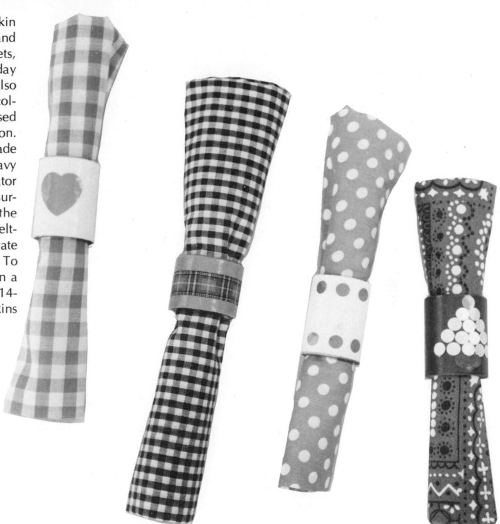

Prequilted Pot Holders

Should there by any material left over from the reversible placemats, it could be used to make matching pot holders in kettle or oblong shape. These too can be colorfully decorated using iron-on tape.

MATERIALS
reversible quilted fabric pieces
bias tape
scissors
sewing machine
iron-on tape
iron

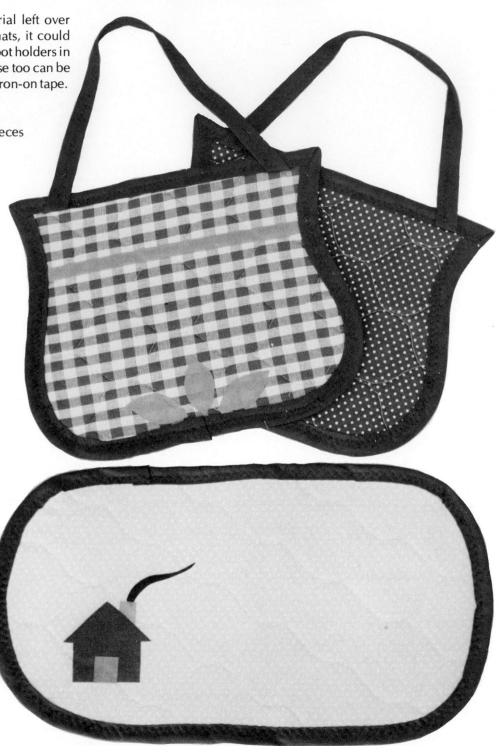

DIRECTIONS

1. Cut the shape for the pot holder from the quilted fabric, following the pattern.
2. Cut iron-on tape designs from patterns and press in place.
3. Bind the edges with bias tape. If making the kettle shape, add strips of bias tape for handles and slip under the edge of the binding before stitching.

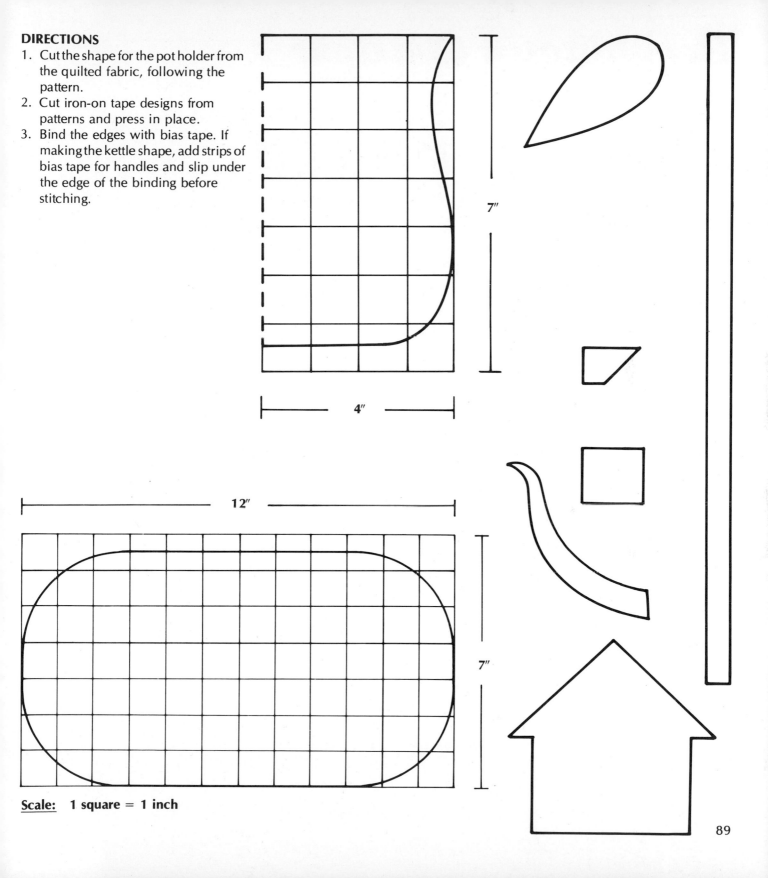

7"

4"

12"

7"

Scale: 1 square = 1 inch

89

Needlepoint Coasters

Colorful needlepoint coasters, stitched with craft yarn on plastic needlepoint canvas, require a minimum of time to complete. Cut the canvas in 3-inch squares and create your design using a favorite needlepoint stitch. To cover the edge of the canvas sew around the sides of the coaster with a whipstitch, using matching or complementary colored yarn. A felt piece, glued onto the back, completes the coaster.

Felt Match Boxes

Felt and glue can be used to transform small match boxes into conversation pieces. For this, a rectangle of felt is cut to cover three sides of the box (leaving one striking surface exposed). Glue the felt in place and add decorations. This could also be done with gummed paper, construction paper, or wrapping paper.

Dried Flower Bookmark

An unusual gift idea is a bookmark displaying delicate dried flowers. Any kind of small garden or wild flowers and leaves can be used, but will need to be placed between layers of paper toweling and pressed in a heavy book. An appropriately sized piece of poster-board must be cut and the flowers arranged in an attractive manner. A tiny dab of glue will help hold the arrangement in place. To seal the bookmark the front is covered with a piece of clear Contac paper, which has been cut slightly larger than the posterboard. Another layer of Contac paper is applied to the back. The edges are pressed firmly around to seal. Excess Contac paper is trimmed to within ¼ inch of the poster-board. A hole is punched near the upper edge and a length of colored yarn is added.

Dried Flower Wall Hanging

A small wall hanging is another way of attractively displaying tiny dried flowers. There are several types of backgrounds that can be used to accentuate the delicate beauty of these small bouquets. Canning jar lids provide a form on which to construct the picture. A fabric circle is cut to fit the circular depression in the center of the lid and glued in place. The dried flowers are arranged on the fabric circle and glued. A tiny bow may be added, if desired. One or more pictures are attached to a wide velvet ribbon for hanging.

Dainty dried bouquets can also be displayed on small sections of wood paneling. The bouquet is arranged, the stems tied with a bow and glued onto the wood background. A picture hanger is attached to the back.

Small dried flower arrangements make a very colorful and lasting gift. There are many little containers which could serve as a holder for the flowers. Metal or plastic boxes, spray can lids, and baskets in appropriate sizes are all possibilities.

Dried Flower Arrangements

Purchased flowers, home dried flowers or weeds, or a combination of these can be used to make arrangements similar to those shown in the picture below. The color of the container should be considered when selecting the flowers for the bouquet. As a rule of thumb, with a colored container, use no more than two colors of dried material. With a white or natural colored container, you will need to limit your color selection to three.

To assemble the arrangement, the bottom half of the container is packed with excelsior. This material allows you to insert the delicate flower stems without breaking and then holds them in place. The flower stems are inserted in the packing, starting in the center and working toward the outer edges. After all the flowers are in place, small bows may be added. If bows are to be placed among the flowers, rather than glued on the basket, a fine wire is attached first, which can then also be pushed into the excelsior.

95

Felt Key Chains and Tags

Hand decorated key chains and tags are an inexpensive bazaar item, both to make and to sell. Felt scraps can be utilized to make a variety of colorful key tags.

MATERIALS
Colored felt pieces
scissors
fabric glue
key ring

DIRECTIONS
1. Cut felt from the pattern.
2. Cut decorative pieces and glue in place using "Tacky" glue. This type of glue is especially good for gluing fabric, as it does not become hard after drying.
3. Add key ring.
4. Glue the two layers together.

Copper Blank Key Holders

A very different, but equally attractive, type of key holder can be made using copper blanks. These copper blanks are readily available at hobby shops in a variety of sizes and shapes.

MATERIALS
copper blanks
model airplane enamel
fine brush, #0 or 00
liquid plastic
key chain

DIRECTIONS
1. Paint the blank with a background color, both on the front and back side.
2. Paint desired design on the front side of the blank. Always allow each color to dry thoroughly before applying the next color.
3. After the design is completed and dried, dip in liquid plastic.
4. Attach the key chain.

Decorated Wooden Spoons

There are a variety of practical and cheerful kitchen gifts that can be offered at a bazaar. Common articles, such as wooden spoons, take on new interest when colorfully decorated. Designs can be added to the spoon handles using permanent felt-tipped markers or enamel paint. Both of these paints are dishwasher safe.

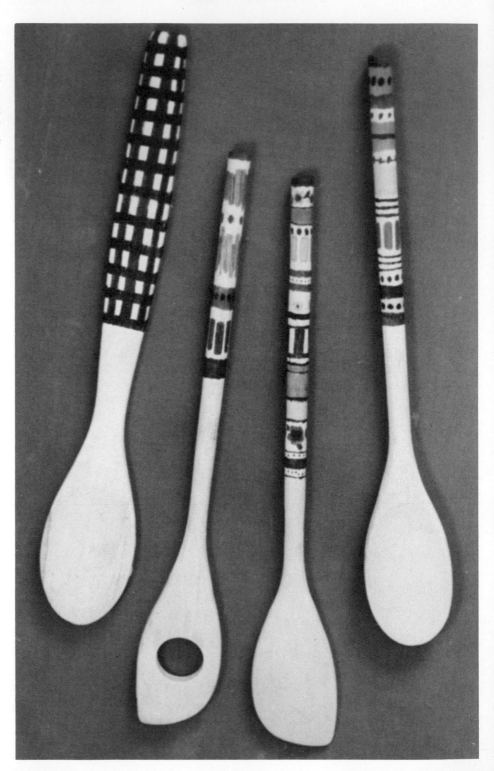

Wooden Trivet

A wooden trivet is a particularly unique item and the type of project that would appeal to someone who has access to, and enjoys working with, a table saw. Part of the beauty of these trivets is the natural wood grain and the variation of the color tones.

MATERIALS
1 dowel, 4 feet long, 1 inch in diameter
table saw
sandpaper
waxed paper
carpenter's glue
felt, 6 by 6 inches

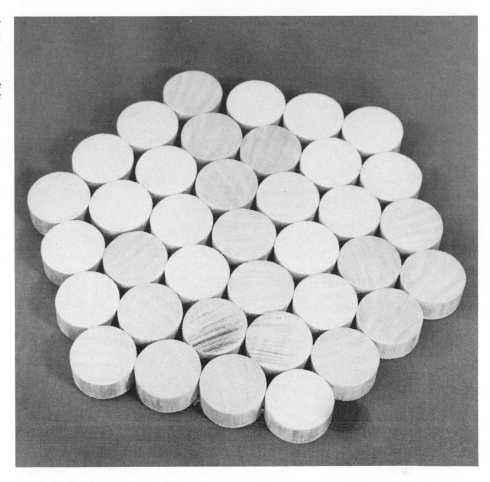

DIRECTIONS
1. Cut the dowel into slices, using the table saw. You will need thirty-seven slices for one trivet.
2. Sand any rough edges.
3. Lay a piece of waxed paper on the working surface. It can be easily removed from the trivet after the glue has dried.
4. Begin gluing the slices together, in this fashion:
   Row 1: 4 slices.
   Row 2: 5 slices.
   Row 3: 6 slices.
   Row 4: 7 slices.
   Row 5: 6 slices.
   Row 6: 5 slices.
   Row 7: 4 slices.
5. When the glue has dried, pull away the waxed paper and cut the felt pieces to fit the back of the trivet. Glue in place.

Cabinetmakers frequently discard small sections of Formica-covered counter tops, such as sink cut-outs. These small pieces provide the raw materials for making some practical kitchen items. The boards can be cut into circles, rectangles, squares or various decorative shapes for use either as trivets or cutting boards. For a finished look, paint the cut edge of the boards using enamel paint.

Wooden Candleholders

The distinctive wooden candleholders in the picture above are not difficult, but do require time. The preformed wooden shapes are readily available at building-supply stores. These pieces are generally sold as shelf supports or as sections for constructing room dividers.

Using a ¾-inch bit, a hole ¾ inch deep is drilled in the center of the top for holding the candle. As an added measure, a small brad can be pounded head first into the center of the hole—the protruding point will give added stability to the candle. The candleholders are finished by either staining or painting with a selection of colored enamels. If enamel is used, each color must be thoroughly dry before another color is applied.

Do-It-Yourself Kit

An ideal gift for the "do-it-yourselfer" is a project in kit form. A patchwork pillow cover kit could be assembled, which could include backing fabric, the required number of cut pieces for the patchwork design, and the directions for making the pillow cover. This idea could be adapted for any kind of stitchery project.

Favorite Recipe Cookbook

A local cookbook need not be an expensive project. Favorite recipes from members of your group or community could be assembled and reproduced on a mimeograph machine, which is by far the least expensive method of reproduction. A sturdy colorful posterboard cover will enhance the appearance of the book. After assembling the pages and the cover, a paper punch is used to make holes, through which yarn can be strung to tie the cookbook together. It is advisable after stringing that a knot be tied in the yarn before the bow is tied. This will prevent the cookbook from coming apart should the bow be accidentally united.

4 Kiddie Corner

When planning a bazaar, consideration should be given to projects that will appeal to children. Small handmade gifts for young people are always in demand. Youngsters also enjoy shopping at a bazaar for small, inexpensive toys and goodies to buy for themselves or a friend; the bazaar becomes more enjoyable for the youngster, and, as a result, more enjoyable for the accompanying adult.

Decorated Doughnuts

Decorated doughnuts are sure to delight young shoppers. These confectionary characters are made from cake doughnuts, popsicle sticks, and frosting. To prevent the doughnuts from breaking first insert a knife through one side, going beyond the hole into the opposite side. Place the popsicle sticks in the doughnuts and lay them on a cookie sheet lined with waxed paper. Prepare an adequate amount of butter cream or decorate icing for use in frosting and decorating the doughnuts. First, frost the top and side of the doughnut, then add the features, using colored icing. Gum drops, colored candies, raisins, and chocolate chips are other decorating possibilities. After the icing has set, place the doughnuts in individual plastic bags and tie them closed.

Character Pencils

Pencils with personality are both practical and fun. Amusing characters can be created from fake fur, cotton, yarn, and feathers. The addition of jiggly eyes and felt features can serve to make them even more lovable.

Some characters can be made in the shape of a cylinder and slipped over the end of the pencil, while others will need to be glued into place. These fuzzy decorations are especially appealing to children because they love to feel the soft textures. An added feature is that these cuddly playthings can also be used as puppets, with the pencil serving as the holder.

Rock Candy Suckers

Children particularly enjoy rock candy suckers because they are so entirely different from other kinds of candy. They are intrigued by the crystal formations and unusual shapes of the suckers. The following recipe is easy and yields roughly a half dozen candies.

MATERIALS
1 cup water
4 cups sugar
saucepan
stove
small glass jars
bamboo skewers, about 4 inches long
small wooden beads
glue

DIRECTIONS
1. Combine one cup water and two cups sugar in a saucepan and stir until all the sugar has dissolved.
2. Place pan over medium heat and begin adding the remaining two cups of sugar. Continue heating and stirring until the solution is completely clear.
3. Pour the sugar solution into small glass jars and insert bamboo skewers. The crystals will begin forming on the skewer after several hours.
4. Each day, remove the skewers and reheat the solution to dissolve the crystals that have formed on the sides of the jars. Cool the solution to lukewarm before adding the skewers again. This will prevent melting the crystals already formed on the sticks. The crystals in the photograph required approximately three days to ''grow.''
5. When the crystals have grown to the desired size, remove from the solution, allow to dry, and then glue a small wooden bead to the end of each skewer.

You may also wish to experiment with colored rock candy (by adding food coloring to the sugar solution) or with brown rock candy (by using brown sugar instead of white).

Clothespin and Cork Puppets

Small character dolls or puppets can provide creative play experiences for youngsters. Because of the detail involved in making these toys, more time will be required for this project; however the expenses are minimal.

Straight clothespins, because of their shape, are easily transformed into human characters. The rounded end is perfect for the head and the straight portion becomes the body. Bottle corks may also be used in making character people. In this case, a child's finger will serve as the body portion of the puppet.

The faces of both kinds of puppets should be painted on before dressing. The type of character chosen will determine the kind of fabric to be used for the body covering. Portions of the wooden soldier shown were painted, but, in all other cases, the puppets were dressed in felt. On the cork dolls, the felt was glued around the bottom edge of the cork, providing the clothing as well as a cylinder for the finger. Any other desired details could then be added.

Bead and Fabric Puppets

Fanciful wooden puppets are made from children's brightly colored stringing beads and bits of fabric and trim. The shape of the bead suggests the type of character to be created. A ¾-inch-deep finger hole should be drilled, using a ¾-inch bit, in the bottom side of the puppet. This may mean simply enlarging the stringing hole or making a new one on the side of the bead. The puppet is brought to life by the use of paint, jiggly eyes, felt, and any other materials suitable for the particular character. To complete the finger puppet a cone of fabric and glue is made inside the finger hole.

Yarn Dolls

The trio of yarn dolls in the photograph are unique in that they have their own display stands. These dolls would make delightful table or display decorations for a child's party. The following materials are for one doll.

MATERIALS

32 strands of yarn, 12 inches long (or black for witch, orange for pumpkin man, or white for snow lady)

35 strands of yarn, 5 inches long (same color as above)

Styrofoam ball, 1½ inches in diameter

30 strands of black yarn, 5 inches long (for witch only)

matching yarn for tying

jiggly eyes

green, red, and black felt

black construction paper for pumpkin man

glue

chenille stick, 5 inches long, for witch

plastic broom straws, 1½ inches long, for witch

masking tape for witch

orange feather for pumpkin man

white beads for snow lady

red calico, 4 by 4 inches, for snow lady

red felt, 6 by 2½ inches, for snow lady

wire coat hanger, 10-inch length

needle

thread

DIRECTIONS

1. Place center of long yarn strands over the Styrofoam ball. Arrange the strands to cover the ball and tie at "neck" with matching yarn.

2. Gather the shorter strands, which are the arms, and tie at each end with matching yarn.

3. Divide the long strands, sixteen in front and sixteen in back, below the neck, slip in the yarn arms, and tie at the "waist."

4. Decorate the dolls as follows:

   Witch

   Glue extra yarn strands on top of head for hair. Add jiggly eyes, a green felt triangle for the nose, and a red felt mouth. Cut the hat (see pattern) from black construction paper. Form a cone and glue the edges together. Insert cone into hat brim and glue. Place the hat on the witch's head, using small drops of glue to hold it in place. Cut cape, using pattern from black felt, and place on doll with slit down the front. Tuck front and back ends under the waist tie or tack them down. Make the broom, using the chenille stick, and attach broom straws with glue. Then wrap the joint with masking tape and glue to front of cape.

   Pumpkin man

   Cut hat, according to pattern, from black construction paper and glue together. Add orange feather and glue in place on head. Glue on black triangles for eyes and nose and a black mouth. The cape for the pumpkin man is made in the same manner as the one for the witch. It is attached to the doll in the same manner also.

   Snow Lady

   Glue white beads on black felt triangles, then glue onto head. Add red felt nose and mouth. Cut the hat from red calico and gather the edge to make a puffy cap. Glue onto head. Cut apron from red felt, trim with pieces of calico or lace, and place on doll. Place the straps over the shoulders, cross in back, and tack to apron sides under the arms.

5. Bend the end of the wire in a semicircle, then fold the remaining wire upward. Place the doll on the wire, running it through the center of the doll up into the Styrofoam ball.

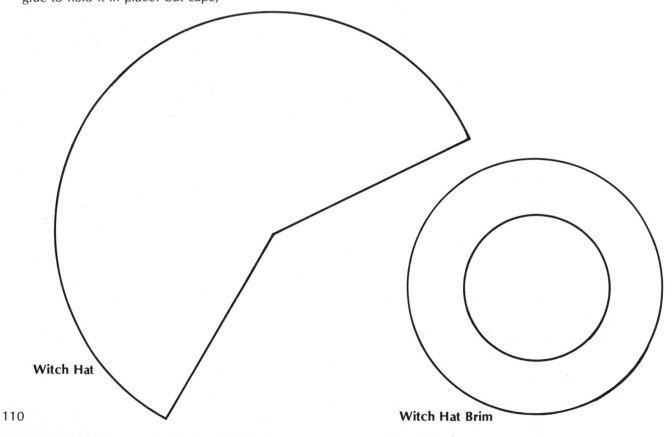

Witch Hat

Witch Hat Brim

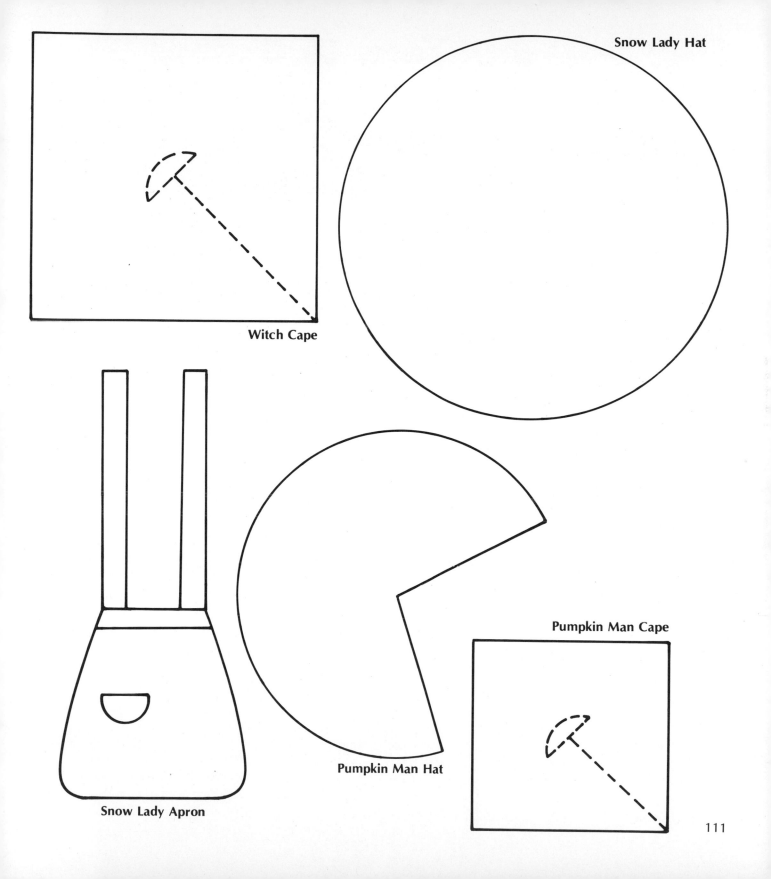

Witch Cape

Snow Lady Hat

Snow Lady Apron

Pumpkin Man Hat

Pumpkin Man Cape

111

Rag Doll and Yarn Doll

Most children, especially the younger ones, enjoy having a doll that they can carry around with them. A small yarn doll is the perfect size to tuck in a pocket or purse. A larger rag doll could become a favorite bedtime friend. Both of these dolls are soft and cuddly and are easy to make.

MATERIALS FOR LITTLE YARN GIRL
22 strands yellow yarn, 10 inches long
wooden bead, 1 inch in diameter, with
  ½-inch hole
yarn for tying
model airplane enamel
paint brush, #0 or 00
glue
calico fabric
needle
thread

DIRECTIONS

1. Gather the yarn strands and slip them through the bead hole.
2. Apply glue to the bead, fold yarn over, and glue in place for hair. Trim off a section of the front for bangs.
3. Take three strands from each side below the bead and braid for arms. Tie at the ends and at the waist.
4. Divide the remaining sixteen strands for the legs. Each group of eight will be braided for each leg. (Note that this will be an uneven braid—three strands, three strands, and two strands.) Tie at the feet.
5. Gather a small piece of calico for an apron and tack in place under the arms.
6. Paint facial features on the bead.

MATERIALS FOR RAG DOLL

gingham, 20 by 11 inches
scissors
sewing machine
Dacron batting
needle
thread
65 strands of yarn, 15 inches long
1 yard of checked ribbon, 1 inch wide
red and blue felt
glue
gingham, 12 by 6 inches
yarn

DIRECTIONS

1. Cut two doll pieces, using the pattern, from the gingham.
2. Starting near the top of the head, stitch around the doll, using a ½-inch seam allowance. Leave the last few inches open.
3. Trim corners and turn right side out. Stuff the doll with Dacron batting and stitch closed.
4. Tack the yarn strands to the top and back of the head.
5. Gather the strands on each side and, with the checked ribbon, tie into a pony tail at each side.
6. Cut blue felt circles for eyes and red circles for cheeks and mouth. Glue these into place.
7. Take the remaining piece of gingham and stitch down ½ inch on each edge of the long sides. Run a length of yarn through the casing on one side. Gather the material and tie the apron around the neck.

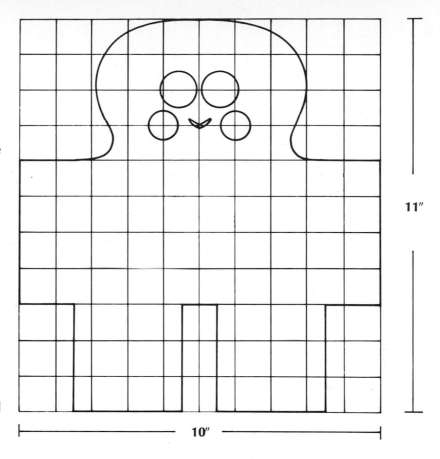

11″

10″

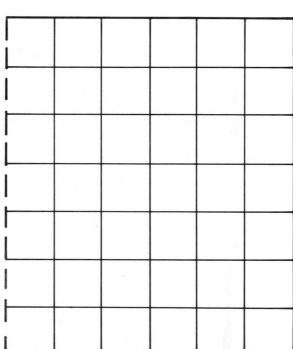

Scale: 1 square = 1 inch

Dotted Line Indicates Fold

113

Apple Dolls

Apple dolls are very unique in appearance. The brown, wrinkly texture of the dried apple is very suggestive of make believe characters. This is one place where you can let your imagination run wild in creating eerie or whimsical creatures.

MATERIALS

apples
paring knife
apple corer
tongue depressors
glue
beads
Dacron batting
felt
fabric
construction paper

DIRECTIONS

1. For each character peel and core an apple, then carve in the main facial features, such as eyes, nose, and mouth. Coring the apple will speed the drying.
2. Set aside the carved apple and let it dry for about one week. You will notice the apple become brown and shriveled.
3. After the drying is complete, glue a tongue depressor in the core opening. The end of the tongue depressor will serve as a handle to hold the puppet.
4. Add desired details such as beads for eyes and teeth, and Dacron batting for hair, moustache, or beard.
5. Dress each character with felt, fabric, and construction paper.

Pom-Pom Creatures

Snuggly pom-pom creatures are sure to be favorites with young children. The only limitation in making these adorable toys is your imagination. In case you're wondering, it is far less expensive to make your own pom-poms than it is to purchase ready-made ones, and there are two types of pom-pom makers on the market, both of which work equally well and which can be purchased at dime stores.

MATERIALS FOR BUG

pom-pom 2 inches in diameter
pom-pom 1½ inches in diameter
glue
felt
scissors
jiggly eyes
artificial flower stamens

DIRECTIONS

1. Glue large and small pom-poms together.
2. Cut legs from felt, according to pattern.
3. Glue on legs, eyes and the artificial flower stamen for the antennae and proboscis (tongue).

MATERIALS FOR BIRD

pom-pom, 1½ inches in diameter
pom-pom, ½ inch in diameter
glue
felt
scissors
jiggly eyes
feather

DIRECTIONS

1. Glue large and small pom-pom together.
2. Glue on feet and wings, cut according to pattern.
3. Add jiggly eyes and small beak cut from felt.
4. For finishing touch, add tail feather.

MATERIALS FOR BEAR

pom-pom, 3 inches in diameter
2 pom-poms, 2 inches in diameter
pom-pom, ½ inch in diameter
glue
felt
scissors

DIRECTIONS

1. Glue the two medium-sized pom-poms onto the larger one to form the ears.
2. Glue small pom-pom on the front for the nose.
3. Cut felt circles for eyes and nose, and a red tongue shape. Glue in place.
4. The bear in the photograph has a handle of yarn. This was the end of the yarn used in tying the pom-pom when it was made. A length of yarn could be glued on, if the ends have already been cut off.

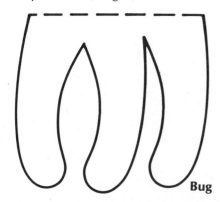

Bug

Wing

Foot

Bean Bags

Bean bags are always popular toys with children, and they are an excellent way of using up fabric scraps. They can be made in most any size or shape, depending upon the material available. Either animals or objects in keeping with a holiday theme are good choices as subjects for bean bags.

MATERIALS FOR EGG
quilted fabric, 7 by 9 inches
lace, rickrack, or other edgings
scissors
sewing machine
needle
thread
dried beans or unpopped popcorn

DIRECTIONS
1. Cut two egg shapes, using the pattern given.
2. Decorate the front piece with strips of lace, rickrack, or edgings. Stitch to the edge of the egg shape.
3. With right sides together, stitch around the edge, using a ½-inch seam allowance. Leave the last few inches open. Turn right side out.
4. Fill the bean bag with dried beans or unpopped popcorn and stitch closed.

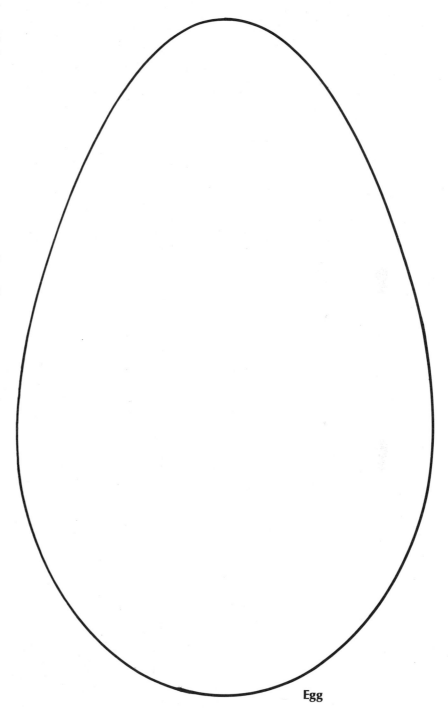

Egg

The hippo bean bag was made in bas-
ically the same manner. The pumpkin is
made from felt and was top-stitched.
Patterns for all the bean bags are given.

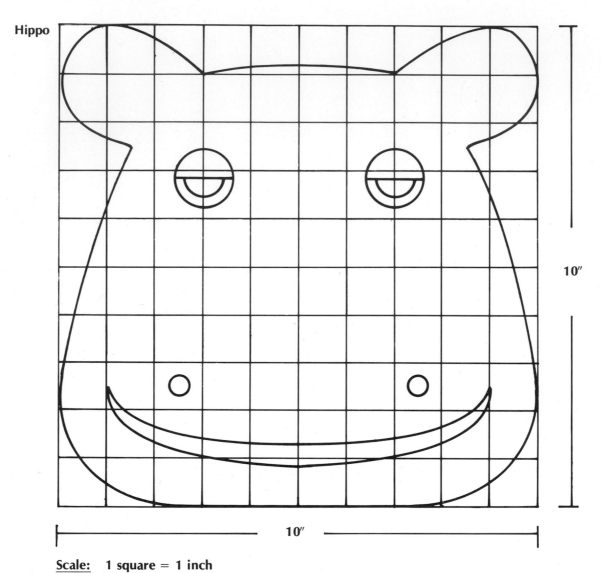

Hippo

10″

10″

<u>Scale:</u> **1 square = 1 inch**

Pumpkin

Cat and Dog Pillows

Any child would love the have an animal pillow all his own. The gingham dog and the calico cat, either singly or as a pair, are sure to be popular items at the kiddie corner. The following materials are for one pillow.

MATERIALS
gingham, 14 by 14 inches
calico, 14 by 14 inches
felt and other fabric scraps
2 buttons, 1½ inch in diameter
straight pins
scissors
sewing machine
needle
thread
Dacron batting

DIRECTIONS
1. Cut all pieces required from fabric, using the patterns.
2. Pin facial feature pieces in place, then machine-appliqué. Use lines of zigzag stitching to form the cat's whiskers. Attach button eyes on dog.
3. Pin ears in place, lay them on the face area, and match the edges with the edge of the face fabric. Lay back piece on top, pin, and stitch around the edge, leaving the last few inches open.
4. Turn right side out, fill with Dacron batting, and stitch closed.

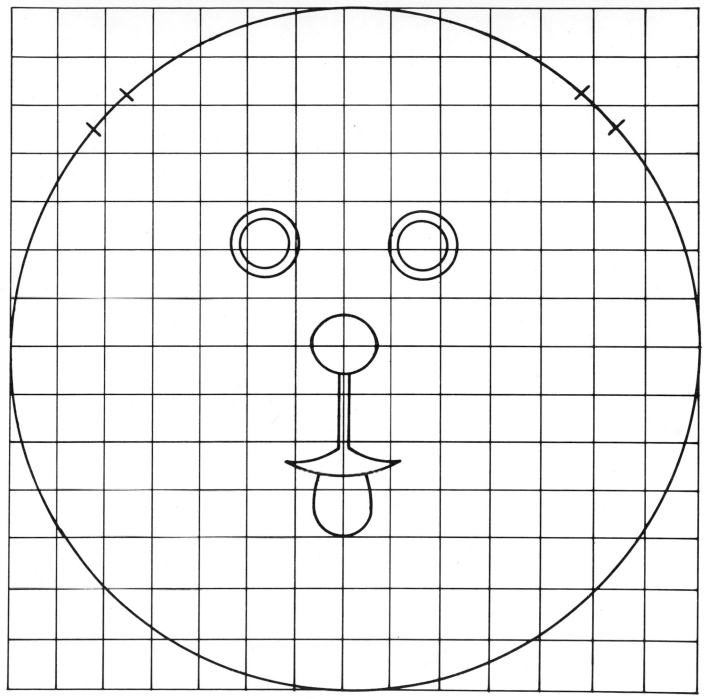

Scale: **1 square = 1 inch**

Dog

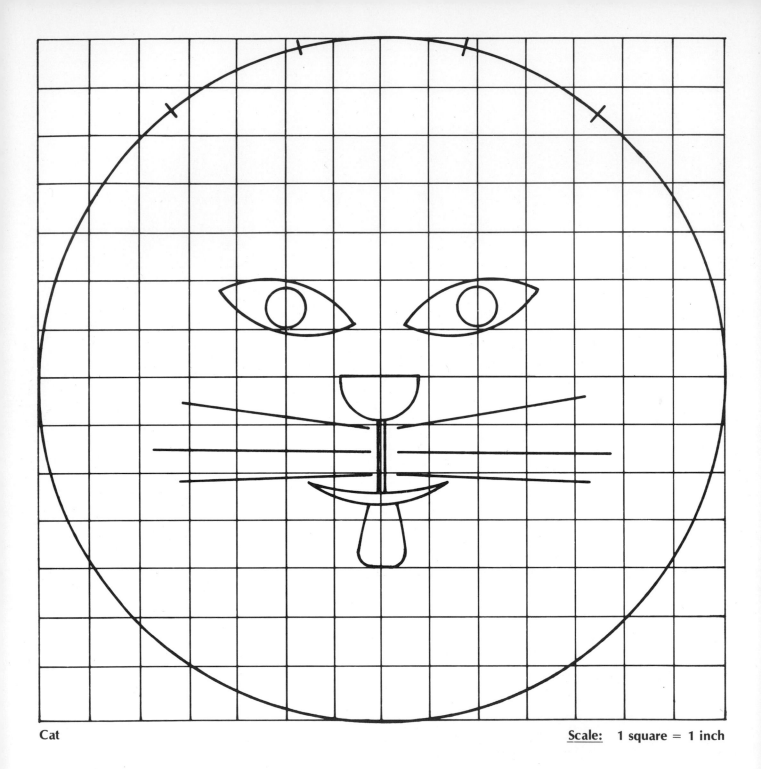

Cat

<u>Scale:</u>   1 square = 1 inch

122

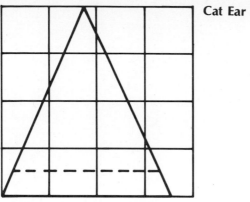

Cat Ear

<u>Scale:</u> 1 square = 1 inch

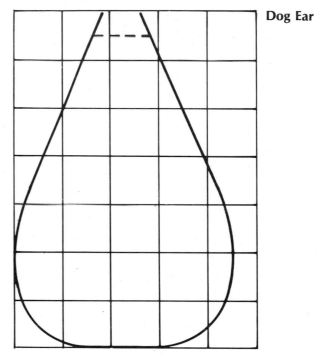

Dog Ear

<u>Scale:</u> 1 square = 1 inch

Here are two more animal pillow patterns for youngsters. These are popular selling items and help decorate the booth, as well.

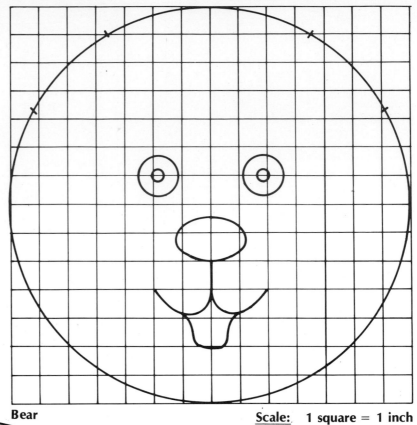

Bear

<u>**Scale:**</u> **1 square = 1 inch**

124

Ear

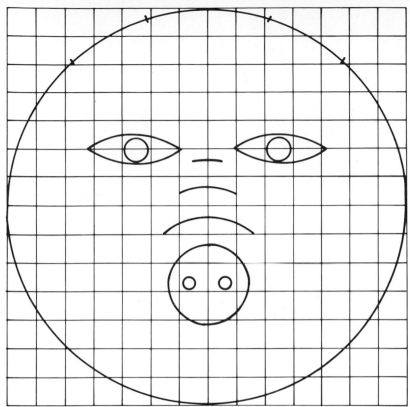

Pig   <u>Scale:</u>   1 square = 1 inch

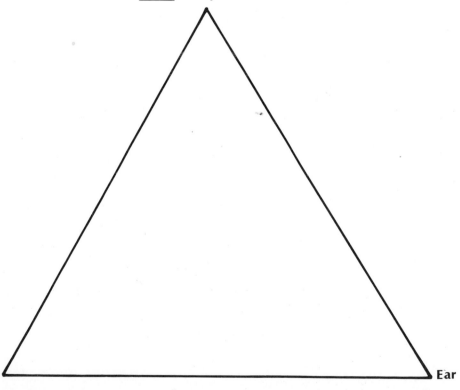

Ear

125

Quilted and Vinyl Bibs

Appropriate fabric remnants will find new life when used for making baby bibs. Most any kind of heavy fabric can be used, provided it is easily cleaned. The bib on the right in the photograph is made from washable quilted fabric, and the other bib is cut from vinyl that can be wiped clean with a damp cloth. The materials given here are enough for one bib.

MATERIALS FOR QUILTED BIB

quilted fabric, 12 by 12 inches
scissors
bias tape
sewing machine

DIRECTIONS

1. Cut the bib from the quilted fabric, according to the pattern.
2. Bind the neck portion of bib with bias tape, top-stitching with a zigzag stitch.
3. Bind the outer edge of the bib, leaving about 12 inches at each end to use for ties.

MATERIALS FOR VINYL BIB

vinyl, 16 by 14 inches
scissors
iron-on tape
pressing cloth
iron
gripper snappers

DIRECTIONS

1. Cut the bib from the vinyl, according to pattern.
2. Cut iron-on tape in any desired pattern. When applying this tape to vinyl, cover with a pressing cloth before ironing. Lay pieces in place, cover, press until tape sticks, then turn the bib over and press on the back side.
3. Attach gripper snappers to neck ends.

Quilted Bib

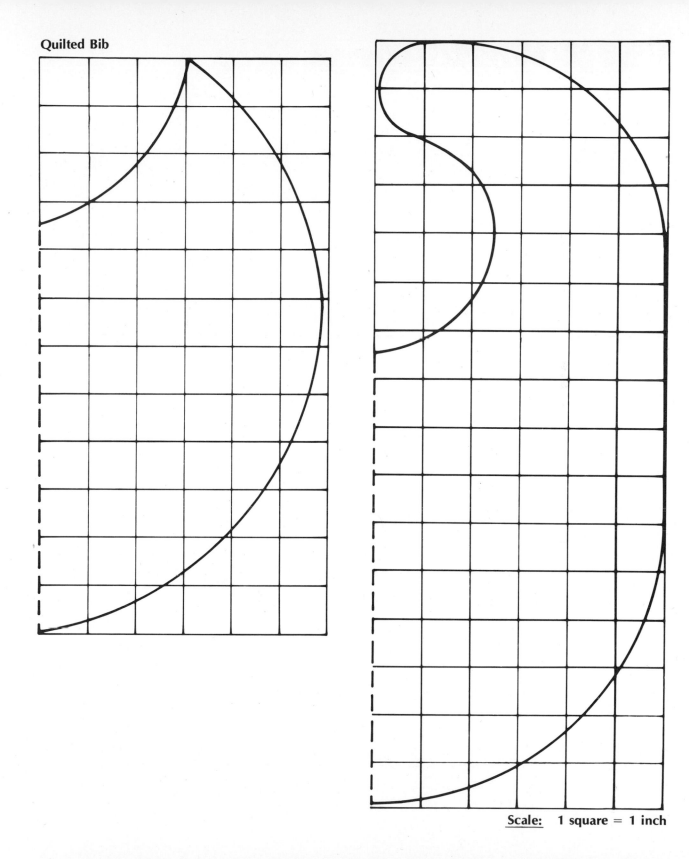

<u>Scale:</u>   1 square = 1 inch

Vinyl Work Apron

Vinyl can also be used to make an ideal children's work apron. It is good for use in such activities as painting, cooking, and gardening. The two front pockets are handy for carrying necessary tools. The following materials are enough for one apron.

MATERIALS

vinyl, 18 by 23 inches
vinyl, 9 by 7 inches, in another color
scissors
sewing machine
tissue paper

DIRECTIONS

1. Cut the apron from the larger piece of vinyl according to the pattern. Cut the pocket section from the second color of vinyl.
2. Cut 1-inch strips from main color of vinyl. These will be used for the side and neck ties, and also for the pocket trim.
3. Stitch trimming strip near the top and down the center of the pocket section. When appliquéing vinyl on vinyl, it may be necessary to lay a piece of tissue paper between the presser foot of the machine and the vinyl. Some types of vinyl do not slide easily, which makes it difficult to get an even seam. The tissue paper will slide easily and can be pulled away after stitching.
4. Stitch pocket section to apron.
5. Attach ties at neck and sides.
6. Cut a 1-inch strip from the second vinyl color and appliqué across the top of the apron.

Dotted Line Indicates Pocket Placement

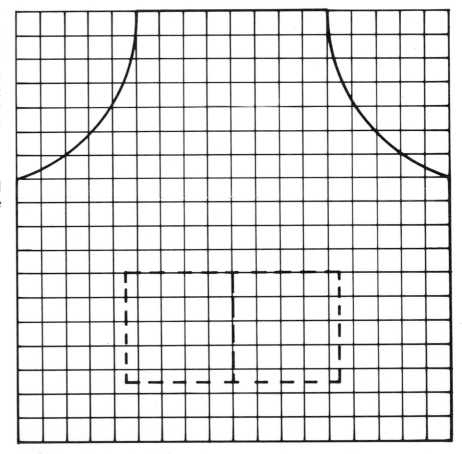

Scale: 1 square = 1 inch

Wooden Puzzles

Puzzles are always welcome toys for children. To make a child's puzzle a simple drawing of something familiar to a child should be used. An easy way is to page through a youngster's coloring book for inspiration. Several kinds of wood could be used to make the puzzles. In the photograph the pony is cut from ½-inch pine shelving and the pig from pressed hardboard (Masonite). Another possible material is ¼-inch plywood. The design can be drawn on the wood and cut along the outline using a jigsaw. The picture should now be cut in pieces to form the puzzle. Each piece should be sanded and painted with lead-free enamels on both sides. This type of puzzle is more challenging than a tray puzzle, because it can be done from either side, but the pieces are not reversible. These wooden puzzles are great fun and can be educational as well.

Horse

Pig

Wooden Toys on Wheels

Moving wooden toys are always favorite playthings; things on wheels fascinate children. Patterns in the actual size of the duck and car are given to aid in making these toys. The materials given here are for one toy.

MATERIALS
pine shelving, ½-inch
jigsaw
wooden dowel, 1 inch diameter
sandpaper
wood stain
paint brush
paper towels or soft cloth
drill
⅛-inch bit
4 brads, 1 inch
4 small metal washers
hammer

DIRECTIONS
1. Cut the toy shape from the pine shelving, with a jigsaw, using the pattern.
2. Cut ½-inch slices from the dowel for the wheels.
3. Sand all edges of the toy and wheels.
4. Stain the pieces by painting with the stain and then wiping dry with paper towels or soft cloth.
5. Drill a hole in the center of each wheel. Be sure to drill the hole straight through the center of the wheel, or the toy will not roll properly.
6. Assemble the toy by inserting the 1-inch brad through the center of each wheel, adding a small metal washer and nailing into the toy.

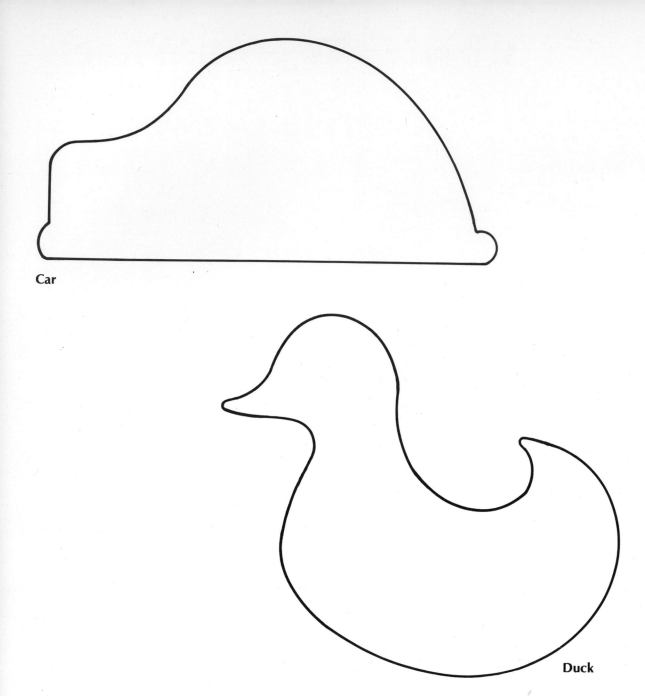

Car

Duck

Metric Conversion Table

LINEAR MEASURE

1 inch = 1,000 millimeters = 2.54 centimeters

12 inches = 1 foot = 0.3048 meter

3 feet = 1 yard = 0.9144 meter

SQUARE MEASURE

1 square inch = 6.452 square centimeters

144 square inches = 1 square foot = 929.03 square centimeters

9 square feet = 1 square yard = 0.8361 square meter

Alphabet and Numbers

Use these letters and numbers to spell out any message you choose for the fabric wall hanging on page 30, or for any project that would be enhanced by lettering.

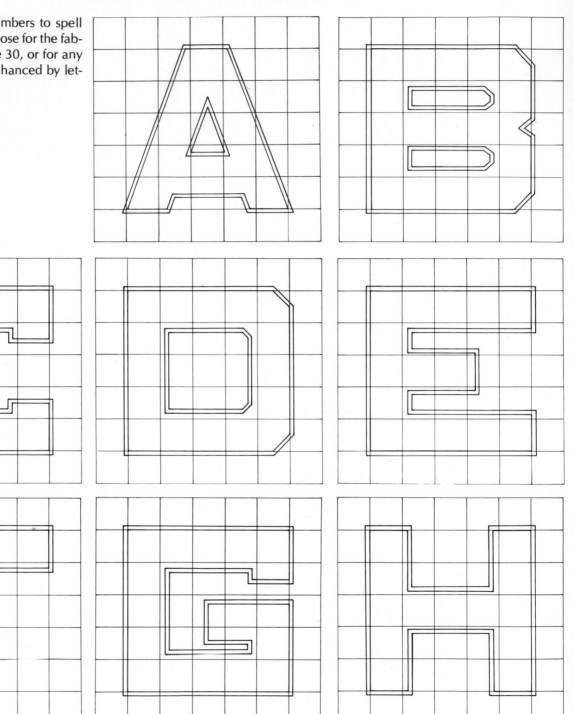

137

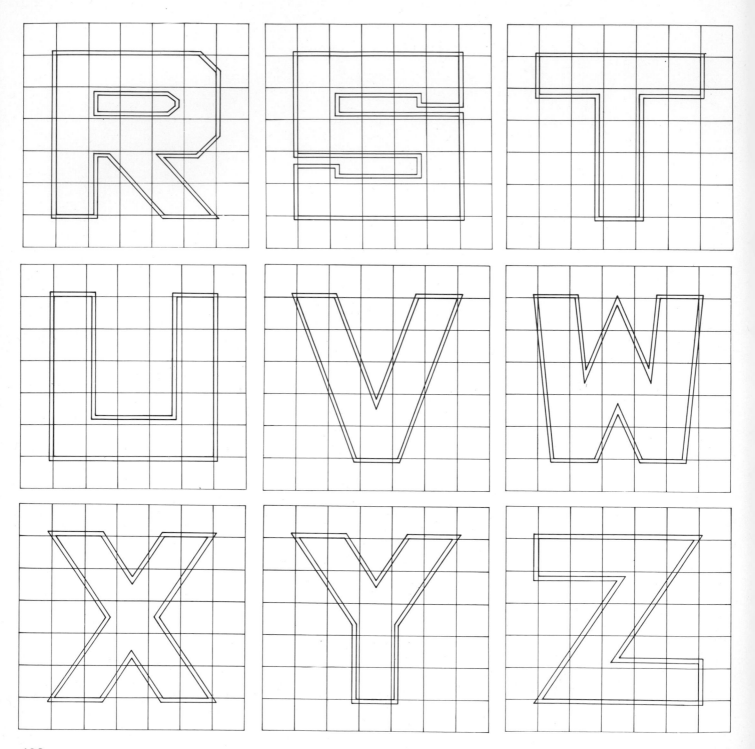

138

139

Cut-Out Grid

This network of 1-inch squares can be
used to enlarge the patterns in the book.
See instructions on page 14.

Cut-Out Graph Paper

Use this graph paper to plot your own
designs for cross-stitch projects.

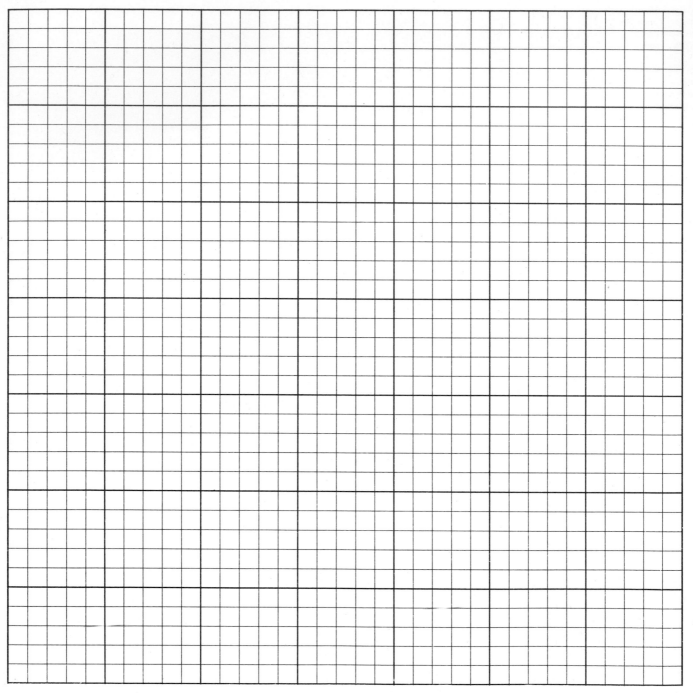

Index